ALFRED WATKINS

ALFRED WATKINS

A Herefordshire Man

by

Ron Shoesmith

LOGASTON PRESS 1990

LOGASTON PRESS
Little Logaston Woonton Almeley
Herefordshire HR3 6QH

First published by Logaston Press 1990
© Copyright Ron Shoesmith 1990

ISBN 0 9510242 7 2

Set in 10/13 pt New Baskerville by Logaston Press
Printed in Britain by Billings and Sons Worcester

To the Watkins family
for all their help and encouragement

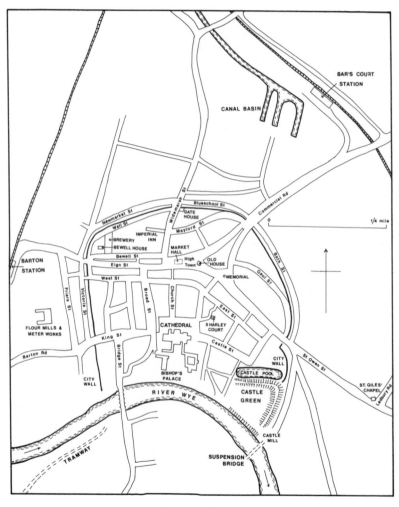

Watkins' Hereford

Contents

Acknowledgements

I would like to record my most grateful thanks to the following people and organisations without whose help this book would never have been written. To the Hereford Public Library, and especially Robin Hill, for access to their large collection of books and photographs concerning Alfred Watkins; to the City Museum for permission to use some of their prints and to illustrate Watkins' photographic apparatus; to the County Record Office for much advice and assistance; to the Registrar of Births, Marriages and Deaths for permission to examine his records; to Godfrey Davies for providing many personal recollections and allowing me to make use of his scrap books; to the Herefordshire Photographic Society for permission to quote from their records; to the Woolhope Club also for permission to quote from their records; to Ken Hoverd, who produced the excellent photographs which are used in this book, often from old prints and glass-plate negatives and to the various people who allowed us to photograph their houses; to my publishers for their unfailing good humour as we approached agreed deadlines and for their help and assistance throughout the project; and finally to the Reverend Felix Watkins and his wife for their help and encouragement and to him and to Dr. Peter Lambert for permission to quote from Allen Watkins' biography of his father.

Introduction

This is not a biography—it is a series of chapters based on the life and times of Alfred Watkins, miller, brewer, archaeologist, photographic innovator and inventor, originator of the ley line theory and a leader of public opinion in his home town of Hereford.

A first-hand account of his life was written by his son Allen some twenty years ago. In it he wrote of the father he knew, respected and loved and it would be presumptuous of me to even attempt to improve on this work. However, Allen's book was published as a limited edition of only three hundred and twenty-five copies and has long been out of print.

1985 was the fiftieth anniversary of Alfred Watkins' death and the BBC in the Midlands took the opportunity to produce a half hour programme 'Mornin' Mr. Watkins' as a tribute to this world-famous Herefordian. But a television programme is seen once and then only dimly remembered.

About the same time, and after much deliberation, Hereford City Council decided to mark the anniversary by naming a street after him. They eventually chose a small, narrow passageway leading from Tesco's supermarket to Widemarsh Street, known locally as Black's Passage, and the sign Watkins Passage was eventually erected. Watkins' daughter, Marion, did not think much of this idea, especially as it was apparently an attempt to save on the cost of a plaque, and she voiced her objections to the Hereford Times! The council reconsidered; the offending street name was removed, and a suitable plaque was eventually unveiled on the wall of 5 Harley Court, where Watkins had lived for many years.

But surely Alfred Watkins, one of Hereford's most famous sons, deserves more than this?

This book, therefore, is written as a small tribute to a man who, although he died before I was born, has provided much of the basic framework for archaeological research within both the county and the city. As Director of the City Archaeological Unit I have followed in his footsteps many times—for several years our office was in Bewell House where we excavated the gardens of what had been the Watkins' family home; we also excavated in places where he had suggested that early defences would be found, and there they were; his records of early Hereford buildings have encouraged us to find others. Throughout the county we make use of his photographs which provide the earliest permanent record of events, buildings and monuments. We constantly refer to his books and the many articles he wrote. Without people like Alfred Watkins, with a long life of selfless service to the county he loved, this country would be a far poorer place.

Ron Shoesmith
Dormington
September 1990

1

Home Life

When Charles Watkins, Alfred's father, arrived in Hereford in 1845 he came to a city which was still dragging itself out of the Middle Ages. The main shopping and residential areas were still more or less bounded by its ancient city walls, although the gates had been demolished some fifty years previously. But this was a period of change. Stage coaches had begun to make travel feasible, not just in the local area but as far afield as Liverpool and London. It was, however, still out of the reach of the ordinary man, for the fare to London was £1 inside and 10 shillings outside for a journey that took fifteen hours or more.

The roads were still poor and incapable of carrying heavy loads, and on his arrival Charles Watkins would have seen the final phases of construction of the Hereford to Gloucester canal. It had taken forty-nine years to complete although it had been open from Gloucester to Ledbury since 1798. (The canal basins are now lost underneath Jewson's timber yard but traces of the canal itself can still be seen in the north-eastern parts of the city.)

He would also have seen the terminus of the horse-drawn tramway on the south side of the river close to the Wye Bridge. This was relatively new, for the final stages had only been completed in 1829. The tramway joined the city to the Newport canal at Abergavenny and together with the canal provided the most economic means of bringing coal to Hereford and of exporting the produce of the county to the vast markets of Bristol, Gloucester and London.

The canal basin at Hereford, the terminus of the Gloucester to Hereford canal, which was opened in 1845

Charles Watkins was born in Mitcheldean, a small town on the edge of the Forest of Dean in Gloucestershire, on 21 January 1821. He was of yeoman stock, his father being a small farmer and, apparently, a carrier which, in the period before the railways arrived, was a trade of some considerable importance. His father would have used long, hooded wagons with teams of strong horses to transport the countryside produce such as grain, wood and fruit to the markets. Their trade would have allowed the Watkins family a degree of independence uncommon in a rural community. One can, perhaps, assume that the younger members of the family had the rare luxury, virtually unknown outside the landed classes, of being able to travel in their father's wagons to places far outside the forest. Charles continued in the same type of business, for, as a young man, he drove coaches daily between Hereford and Cirencester.

Charles came to Hereford as a single man and became innkeeper of one of the many public houses which were then to be found in

*Charles Watkins with gun, dog and game on the steps at Holmer Park
about 1870 (Bustin, Hereford)*

Eign Street. Before he had been in the city very long, he found himself a wife, Ann Hill. She had been brought to Hereford from Ireland to work in one of the local inns and was thus hardly the ideal choice for an up-and-coming businessman. However the marriage was extremely successful and it is clear that Ann Watkins overcame any prejudice that there may have been in Hereford society concerning her humble beginnings. Charles and Ann had two children, Charlotte and Charles, whilst they lived in Eign Street, then sometime between 1848 and 1850 they moved to what was presumably a larger premises with more potential. This was the Imperial Inn in Widemarsh Street—still not a large establishment, but one which Charles must have felt sure that he could improve and thus make the basis of his fortune.

Charles and Ann Watkins must have appeared to be a typical well-to-do Victorian family for they had a total of ten children between

The Imperial Hotel (as it's now known) in Widemarsh Street where Alfred Watkins was born in 1855. The inn was totally rebuilt at the beginning of the twentieth century (Ken Hoverd, 1990)

1847 and 1860, although the two youngest died in infancy from either diptheria or typhoid. Apart from Charlotte and Charles, Ann, John and Henry were also older than Alfred. He was born on 27 January 1855, the sixth of the eight surviving children, and had two younger sisters, Fanny and Alice.

During the decade before Alfred was born, there had been some changes in the city but the biggest improvements were yet to come. The main event, which was to be the catalyst for all the others, was the arrival of the railway from Newport and Abergavenny, which was opened to Barton Station in 1854. This was followed in rapid succession by the rail links to Shrewsbury, Worcester and Gloucester, with the line to Brecon and south Wales following in 1862.

The Hereford Improvement Act of 1854 led to vast changes in the city whilst Alfred was still being wheeled around in his pram. As an infant he must have seen the almost constant excavations in the streets as mains water and sewage pipes were laid. When his father came to Hereford water had to be obtained from wells or pumps and there was no main sewage disposal system. William Humfrys, born in 1842, gives a vivid impression of the earlier system in his *Memories of Old Hereford* when he said: 'Sewers there were none. In some houses such drain as existed in the house discharged into a pit under the dining room, or some other room on the ground floor, and either sank into the ground or evaporated.'

Alfred was born at the Imperial Inn, and a late nineteenth century description gives some indication of its size and design. It contained a smoke room and one large public bar which had no less than four entrances. To the rear were the kitchen, the back kitchen and a spirit store, whilst in the basement there were stock rooms and a beer cellar. On the first floor they had a large sitting room and, at the rear, two bedrooms. The second floor contained additional attic bedrooms. It may well have been lit by gas, for a gas works was first built in the city in 1836. Behind the building was a long, narrow yard approached from Widemarsh Street through an archway. The yard contained the brewhouse and other sheds and it was here that Charles Watkins produced the various brews which were to make his reputation with native Herefordians.

The educational system in the middle of the nineteenth century operated at two different levels; first there were the charity schools and those attached to the parishes and supported by the various churches. But in addition there was a gradually increasing number of private, fee-paying schools, both day and boarding. Alfred was sent to one of the latter which was conveniently situated in what is now the Farmers Club at the junction of Widemarsh Street and Blueschool Street. This fine timber-framed building is of the late fifteenth or early sixteenth century. Thomas Church (who was Mayor of Hereford in 1636) lived here and probably carried out some renovation in 1626, the date on the side door which gave access through the city wall. At the beginning of the nineteenth century the building was in use as a ladies school being run by a Miss Croucher. She employed the famous artist David Cox for some time as a drawing master at a salary of £100p.a.

In 1865 it was re-established as a boys school by the Reverend W. Bowell M.A. so Alfred must have been one of its first pupils. He was not impressed by it at all, for many years later he told his son that it was 'a shocking bad school where the teaching was perfectly dreadful and I learned absolutely nothing'. However he appears to have taken an early and extensive interest in the building for he noted during a visit in 1920, some fifty years after he had been a pupil, that one of the rooms that was then bare had been panelled when he was at school. In the early 1870's Rev. Bowell moved his school to Chandos House in St. Owen Street where it had the rather grand title of Chandos House Collegiate School. About 1873 Mr. E. Colt Williams, Her Majesty's Inspector of Schools, took over the Widemarsh Street building. He found panelling pulled down and a plaster ceiling destroyed, so reconstructed and decorated the rooms to his own taste. By 1890, the Rev. Bowell had moved back to his original building, by then known as the Gate House, in Widemarsh Street.

Whilst Alfred was young, his father extended his brewing interests and bought the Hereford Brewery in Bewell Street. Although there have been some considerable improvements in this narrow street during the last few years, it does not appear to have ever had any great character of its own. Appearances are deceptive however, and in the mid-nineteenth century, when Alfred Watkins was a young boy walking from his home in the Imperial Inn to his father's newly acquired brewery, the street would have been fuller of interest than it is now. It included several well-established inns including the Rummer Tavern, the Royal Standard, the Weavers Arms and the Bowling Green—the latter being the only one to survive to the present day. There were many small businesses to attract a youngster's attention including a shoemaker, a candle maker, a tailor and a clockmaker, not to mention several dining rooms. Leading off the street to the north were narrow passages which opened out into several courts, such as Sheriffs Court and Fryers Court, containing small half-timbered houses, since demolished as part of a slum clearance programme.

As owner of one of the principal breweries in the city, Charles needed an appropriate residence and it was during the 1860's that

Holmer Park, the house designed and built by Charles Watkins, shortly after it was completed (Butsin, Hereford)

he decided to design and build his own house! This was Holmer Park, now on the northern outskirts of Hereford but then well in the country although sufficiently close to the city for convenience. Rather than buy bricks he dug his own clay pits in the grounds, later utilizing the area as a sunken rose garden. The iron railings which adjoined the gates were originally part of the churchyard railings around St. Paul's Cathedral. Charles Watkins acquired them on one of his occasional visits to London when he found they were being replaced. These railings are thought to have been made of 'wealdon iron' from the local ore in the Weald in Sussex. Very few examples survive to the present day. Although Alfred must have watched this new house grow, this was one area in which he was never to follow in his father's footsteps and design his own house.

In 1870 an unexpected opportunity arose to buy Bewell House at the far end of Bewell Street and adjoining the brewery. It may be that Charles had to sell his new house at Holmer to buy this ideally placed property which, it appears, he made his town residence. Alfred recalled that he had lived in Bewell House as a lad, but apparently for no great length of time.

Bewell House, still a significant part of the streetscape in this part of Hereford having preceded and outlived the brewery, would have been a very impressive town house for the Watkins family. The main floor included a breakfast room, a library, a drawing room and a dining room, togther with a servants' hall, kitchen, scullery, butler's pantry and the usual services. There were four principal bedrooms on the first floor and a further four on the second. The forecourt onto Bewell Street contained stabling which included two stalls, a loose box and a coachhouse with a loft above. Behind the house much of the formal garden was retained although the eastern part was walled off and taken over by the brewery. This was a far cry indeed from the limited accommodation at the old Imperial Inn.

Charles was a typical Victorian entrepreneur and his various businesses expanded rapidly. They must also have been very profitable, for shortly after 1870 he decided to move further out into the countryside and bought the Wisteston Court Estate in the parish of Marden, some six miles north of Hereford. The whole family moved

*In the courtyard at Wisteston Court. This was the home of Watkins' father
from about 1870, but has since been demolished (Alfred Watkins)*

there and many years later Alfred recalled their visits to the summer
Sunday services in Wisteston Chapel where the children could
crouch down, totally out of sight, in the large court pew close by the
door. Wisteston Court included a timber-framed fifteenth century
wing, which probably started its life as an open hall, as well as much
seventeenth century work and may have served as an introduction
to architectural history for the young Alfred. This building has since
been lost—it was already in poor condition when the Royal
Commission on Historical Monuments visited it in 1930. It
continued to deteriorate during the war years and was derelict in
1963 when Pevsner wrote his *Buildings of Herefordshire*. Now all that
remains is a pile of rubble with historic timbers protruding in all
directions.

As the children grew up, the boys were probably all expected to
learn the brewing trade, but it is apparent that not all of them had
the same interest. It was in 1883 that his father decided to admit
Henry, who was reputed to be very clever, into partnership with

him, and from that time the son managed the entire brewery. But he only survived his father by about a year, for in January 1889 he was found drowned in the River Lugg at Lugwardine. Both Charles and Alfred apparently continued to work in one or another of the family businesses, but John became a local farmer in Withington; however he also died relatively young. Alfred's oldest sister, Charlotte, never married. As so often happened in large families, she probably spent most of her youth looking after the younger children during her mother's many pregnancies. However, his other three sisters were all married successfully; Fanny and Alice were married at Lugwardine, the former to Robert Thomas Griffiths, a solicitor of Hay-on-Wye, and the latter to Henry Hill, a gentleman from Dymock. Ann eventually married a member of the Hatton family which had been involved in the tanning business in Hereford for many years.

Charles finally moved to Wilcroft in Bartestree, an eighteenth century mansion of considerable character which he extended to

Wilcroft (Ken Hoverd, 1990)

Ann Watkins at Wilcroft about 1897 when she was 76 (Alfred Watkins)

provide the accommodation he required as a major businessman in the city. The building still survives, some four miles east of Hereford on the Ledbury road, although it is now split into several separate dwellings. He may well have moved to be closer to his son John, who was still at Pomona Farm in the adjoining parish of Withington. He was struck with paralysis in 1885 whilst visiting Llandrindod Wells and from that time onwards was rendered helpless and speechless although he retained his other faculties. He eventually died in 1888 but his widow continued to live at Wilcroft until she died on 16 December 1899. After legacies, the residue of Charles Watkins' estate was split into eight equal parts, one for each of his children. Each share amounted to £1,653, quite a considerable sum of money at that time.

As a young man Alfred Watkins served in the Herefordshire Volunteers which had been formed during the Napoleonic Wars. It was under the control of Colonel Heywood of Hope End in Colwall parish near the Worcestershire border, a house to which Alfred was often invited. He found Hope End a particularly interesting house, or in fact series of houses for it was re-built twice. In the early nineteenth century it had been the home of the famous poetess Elizabeth Barrett-Browning, and Alfred later wrote an article *Elizabeth Barrett and Hope End* for the Woolhope Club *Transactions* in 1925. (The Woolhope Club was devoted to the study of the county of Herefordshire and its adjoining areas, and Watkins was later to become its president.) On his death he left an unfinished manuscript for a book called *The Masefield Country* which included a chapter on Hope End.

The Woolhope Club article gives a rare insight into Alfred's habits and methods of obtaining information. He mentions his friend John Edy Ballard, one of the three talented Ballard brothers—the others being Phillip, the artist, decorating Worcester and Madeley porcelain and later acting as adviser during the Hereford Cathedral restorations only to be murdered in his bed at Tupsley, and Stephen who was responsible for the construction of the Hereford to Ledbury canal. Through his friend John he met the old Mr. Thomas Edy who lived at The Frith, near Ledbury—where

Alfred describes having breakfast of cold beef and perry whilst quizzing the old gentleman about the Barretts. Then, walking in the area he met a bark-stripper who provided details of the demolition of the second Hope End. A little old man walking with sticks added more to the story, as did old Mrs. Pedlingham of Colwall Green who, as a maid at Old Colwall, remembered Miss Barrett and, as an added bonus, Miss Florence Nightingale paying a visit.

One of his visits to the Ledbury area was rather a special one—together with a friend he decided to canoe the full length of the Hereford to Gloucester canal before it finally closed. This was in 1880 and the trip took two days. Swimming and rowing were Alfred's principal sports, but canoeing must also have been included for his grandson still has an inscribed medal that Watkins won at the Bath Regatta in 1878. In later life he was to be closely associated with the Hereford Rowing Club, becoming captain and eventually a vice-president.

It was in 1886, at the age of 31, that Alfred married Marion Mendham Cross. She was the daughter of Charles Cross of The Mall, Brentford in Middlesex, in which town the wedding took place. Cross was a wealthy businessman associated with the soap-making firm of Thomas and Berry Rowe (twins who were reputed to be the originals for Dickens' Cheeryble Brothers). Marion must have found Hereford a great change from Middlesex, and Alfred a totally different type of person to those with whom she had previously mixed. At a much later date his daughter was to describe her father as: 'a bit of a rough diamond to look at. Broad-shouldered and bearded, he wore (winter and summer) suits of Harris Tweed lined with grey flannel, containing fourteen pockets. These pockets were filled with letters, pamphlets, tools, rulers and other paraphernalia. When the coat was almost too heavy to lift, he would empty the paper content in a heap on a deal table in his "den". This room was a scene of apparent chaos, but he could always find everything he wanted.'

Perhaps these multitudinous pockets helped him to entertain his children when they were young, for he was considered to be quite a good amateur conjurer.

23

The newly-weds moved into one of the more pleasant suburbs of Hereford when they took over Sunnyside in Broomy Hill. This is a house of reasonable size in its own grounds and would have been more than satisfactory for the young couple. However, they soon started a family with Allen, who was born in 1889, and Marion, who was born seventeen months later. It was just before Marion was born that the family decided to move to the eastern side of the city where they lived at the rather imposing Vineyard Croft in Hampton Park. This house, with its large gardens which continued right down to the banks of the River Wye, was an ideal place to bring up children and the Watkins stayed there for almost thirty years.

Their new house was in a rather odd historical situation, for it was within the parish known as The Vineyard—surely one of the smallest parishes in the country as it had a population of only thirteen! Alfred was appointed to the honorary position of Overseer for the Poor of this minute parish, a position which could hardly have involved any great effort. The parish, which had originally been a

The drawing room at Vineyard Croft in 1897 (Alfred Watkins)

Vineyard Croft from across the River Wye in 1902 (Alfred Watkins)

A fete in aid of the Herefordshire Volunteers held in the grounds of Vineyard Croft (Alfred Watkins, 1915)

piece of ground belonging to St. Guthlac's Priory, no longer exists as a separate entity.

The house, according to his daughter Marion, was filled with a collection of old English furniture, picked up at moderate prices. The shelves were packed with old and curious books that Alfred fancied. He also collected coarse Staffordshire slip-wares and the pottery designs of the Martin brothers from Southall. Perhaps most evocative were the Arthur Rackham illustrations of Peter Pan, which he hung on the walls. The cellars were used as a dark room for his photographic work which became of ever increasing importance during his long stay at Vineyard Croft.

Garden parties were a regular event in the early twentieth century and the grounds of Vineyard Croft provided an ideal location. During the Great War Alfred and Marion Watkins held several parties to provide funds for the war effort. One fete, in August 1915, raised £71 and 14 shillings, which bought fifteen rifles, bugles and bayonets for the 150 strong Hereford Voluntary Training Corps.

Watkins' wife Marion at Vineyard Croft about 1891 (Alfred Watkins)

The young Allen was more fortunate than his father for he was educated at the Hereford Cathedral School. He was presumably a good scholar for he went on to read Economics at St. John's College, Cambridge, eventually becoming a chartered accountant in London and Cambridge. He followed his father in writing books; compiling one on economics for chartered accountants and others on bridge.

Alfred Watkins started his travels around Herefordshire by horse and gig but changed to a more modern form of transport at the beginning of the twentieth century. He possessed a succession of steam cars—a Gardner-Serpollet, a Stanley and a Pearson-Cox—which, being gearless and noiseless, provided an excellent form of transport for a man whose main interests were his surroundings rather than the road ahead. It is not generally appreciated that the fuel for steam cars was paraffin and that they used more fuel per mile than ordinary petrol cars. They also cost more to manufacture. The main disadvantage, though, was that frequent stops were needed to add water to the boiler and then to get up a head of steam. With steamers, on the old Hereford to Abergavenny road, it was generally understood that a stop would be needed for water, and of course a drink, at the Angel (now sadly closed) and then up the Callow Hill as far as the church for more boiler pressure!

We are indebted to his son for an account of an accident in which his father was involved in 1904. 'He was ascending Bredwardine Hill which is reputed to include a 1 in 3 gradient, but his car, a Stanley, was at that time the best climber on the road and in normal conditions was equal to any hill. Unfortunately conditions were far from normal. The road surface was thick in mud, and the wheels failed to grip. The car moved backwards and father reversed quickly into the hedge, but it was too late, and the car overturned. Driver and passenger were both thrown clear. The passenger, a Hereford man, was virtually unhurt, but father was knocked unconscious with head and leg injuries. He forced himself back into consciousness to gasp instructions to his passenger to open the safety valve quick. The steam was thus allowed to escape and an explosion prevented. He then lapsed back into unconsciousness.

Watkins in his Gardner-Serpollet steam car about 1908

'In those days no ambulances were available in remote country districts. The passenger telephoned the Flour Mills, and the latter sent out their Foden steam wagon with a bed! In this unconventional chariot father was transported to his home at The Vineyard.'

There are few records of Alfred Watkins' tours and visits outside Herefordshire, although it is apparent that he was reasonably well-travelled in England and Wales. He must have visited London several times for he recollected, in an article in the Hereford Times in 1932, 'As a young man I twice had a before-breakfast-dip in a small plunge bath fed by a natural spring, in Strand Lane, just in and out of the chilly water. It was built by the Herefordshire-born Earl of Essex of Elizabeth's time and adjoining it was the old Roman bath fed by the same spring. I think that the Hotel Cecil was built over all this.'

In the late 1880's he visited the Gower, where he surveyed several pigeon houses for an article published in *The Royal Archaeological Journal.* He only went to Cambridge once, to visit his son who was in practice there. He never bothered to visit any of the colleges but spent much of his time at the ancient castle mound. But in a great burst of energy he carried out the necessary research to write and illustrate his book *Archaic Tracks round Cambridge* published in 1930.

His son also records the time he, his sister and their father went with a large party to Klosters, Austria, for the winter sports. Alfred was an accomplished skater, probably partly as a result of the many hours he had spent at his father's roller-skating rink (built during an early interest in this activity) when he was young.

II

Golden Sunlight—The story of the Hereford Brewery

In the early nineteenth century many of the smaller taverns in Hereford were little more than the front rooms of houses where men congregated to talk and drink. They were mainly beer houses—the brew being made in sheds at the rear of the premises with each individual house having its own distinctive flavour. The Imperial Inn, when it was taken over by Charles Watkins, was a typical example, although perhaps a little larger than some of its neighbours. It was, and indeed still is, on the western side of Widemarsh Street almost opposite the junction with Maylord Street. During the nineteenth century Widemarsh Street was one of the busiest streets in Hereford, for it took all the north-south traffic going through the city. The Imperial, half way between the market place in High Town and the site of Widemarsh Gate, was in an ideal position to attract trade. Its position may well have been reinforced by being next to the Mansion House. This had been built by Dr. William Brewster in 1697. It was bought by the city council around 1763 and became the official residence of the mayor, but from 1882 until the new town hall was built in 1904, it was used as council offices.

However, there was substantial competition, for Hereford in the nineteenth century was a city full of public houses. Within the city boundary there were over two hundred and most streets in the centre could boast of several—indeed some crossroads had a pub on each corner! Widemarsh Street was no exception; a few doors down the street from the Imperial was the Black Swan, an ancient

The main thoroughfare through the Imperial Brewery looking north from Bewell Street in 1892. The large building with the chimney is the brew-house and on the right is the vat room

coaching inn. Almost next door to the Imperial, on the way out of town, was the Albion and across the road, on the corner with Maylord Street, stood the Raven, the site of the birthplace of David Garrick in 1716, and a few doors along Maylord Street the Redstreak, presumably named after the cider apple, and later to be called the Golden Cross. Also on the opposite side of the road there were two small drinking houses which were only known by their street numbers—Number 7 and Number 10, although the latter had been known as the New Inn. Along with many other small inns and taverns in Hereford, all these have closed and only the Imperial remains.

The Imperial was extended and totally rebuilt at the beginning of the twentieth century, keeping its original name, although now dignified with the title of hotel. The architect was G.H. Godsell and the facade, a reconstruction of the original half-timbered building, is a fine example of the vernacular revivalism current at that time.

Charles Watkins had a vitality which characterised so many early Victorians; he was not content to be merely the landlord of a relatively small inn in a provincial city—his aspirations were much greater. His son recalled something of this spirit in an article he wrote many years later for the Hereford Times concerning the railway tunnel underneath Dinmore Hill. 'My father told me that a great deal of beer went into the making of that tunnel, and as he had just built his new brewery (he had been up to the Great Exhibition of 1851 and there bought the newest brewing appliances, glorified under the high-sounding name of 'Imperial patent' thus providing a name for his inn and for the larger brewery he built later), he came into most of the supplying. It can be told now, for such days belong to half a century ago, but he mentioned that then, when brewer's yeast, instead distiller's as now, was in demand for bread making, he had often known the cost of malt and hops to be entirely paid by the sale of the now often wasted products, the "barm" and grains.'

He must have been extremely successful as an innkeeper for within twelve years he was sufficiently prosperous to take over the Hereford Brewery. This lay just around the corner from the

Imperial at the western end of Bewell Street where it provided a break between the row of small houses and shops and the large Bewell House.

The Hereford Brewery had been built in 1834 by J.C. Reynolds who had previously started the Fownhope Brewery, some six miles outside the city. Indeed, the initials and date J.R. 1834 were a feature of the keystones of several arches within the complex which survived until the final demolition of the brewery. Charles Watkins bought the premises in about 1858, after they had been closed for some twelve years, but soon restarted production and was able to increase his output substantially from the restricted capacity he had had in the sheds at the rear of the Imperial. He was a man of intense creative energy and immediately began to extend the premises by adding adequate stores for his already large wine and spirit business. It was then that he changed the name from the rather

The cask yard at the rear of the brewery in 1892. In the distance is the spire of All Saints Church

parochial Hereford Brewery to the much grander Imperial Brewery. This was the first of Charles' major enterprises and although he was to expand into several other fields, it is evident that the brewery was the central part of his empire and the one on which he expended much of his time and effort.

As the brewery grew, Charles was able to take over several public houses in Hereford and, in closing their small brewhouses, increase his own outlets. Throughout the 1860's the trade continued to grow until by the end of the decade the brewery was becoming chronically short of room. But the only way that Charles Watkins could expand was by taking over Bewell House together with its extensive formal gardens at the rear. This house had been built over a hundred years earlier in 1724 and, in the early years of the nineteenth century, was the home of Thomas Hardwick, a local solicitor. Between about 1855 and 1870 it was occupied by Francis Henry Thomas Esq., M.A. (Oxon), J.P., D.L., who was described as a fox-hunting man, originally from Monmouthshire. Thomas died in 1870 and Charles seized his opportunity to purchase the property. This enabled him to extend the brewery yard and buildings through to the narrow Wall Street on the north, and eventually to the much more important Blueschool Street, now part of the ring-road. It also provided himself and his family with a considerable town house.

It would have been shortly after the family's move to Bewell House that Charles Watkins decided that Alfred should learn the brewery business—inevitably by starting at the bottom. At a much later date, he remembered his early years at the brewery in an entertaining article in the Hereford Times about the blacksmith's craft. 'As a boy, with the run of my father's brewery, it was in the cooper's and blacksmith shops that I found my spiritual home. The first-named was perhaps in early days the most attractive, with its varied and strange craft-work and sweet smell of oak-chips and shavings. But in this place, where staves were shaved, bellied and trussed up, sharp cutting tools, not to be trusted to small boys, were all about, and it was the same with the rather sterner guardian in the carpenter's domain. So, as I now know, it was the blacksmith's forge that laid the deepest spell on the mind of a young tool-user, for not

The cooper's workshop at the Imperial Brewery (Alfred Watkins)

so easily damaged were the hammers and tongs, cold chisels and punches, and the "Old Cole" who only occasionally had a smithy job to vary his regular engine driving, allowed a little lad to blow up the shred of fire on the hearth, to heat a bit of iron, and hammer it up into any kind of odd shape. And later on the friendly old man put me on to making my apprentice's pair of tongs.'

He would also have worked in the cooper's shop making casks from the native oak. He described this later. 'At my father's brewery there were in the yard great open stacks, like chimneys some twenty-five feet high, of cleft English oak put to season for the coopers to make into casks. The woodmen cleft and sawed them in the rough the right sizes for staves and heads of kilderkins and barrels, each piled in its stack—delightful for a boy to climb up inside!'

Indeed one of his first hobbies was the craft of woodworking for which he had considerable talent. It was an interest even mentioned in his obituary where it was said that surviving pieces showed a high standard of taste and skill. One wonders where these pieces are nowadays.

The brewery offices in Eign Street at the end of the nineteenth century. The ornate building is partly hidden by the extensive advertising boards. The building, now without these great boards, still survives and includes the passageway leading through to Tesco's supermarket

In about 1873 Alfred, then a young man, travelled by horse and gig around Herefordshire on the brewery business. It is apparent that he did not find the business very congenial for he seems to have spent much of his time during his travels talking to those he met on the road and taking photographs, rather than visiting the back street public houses in the small county towns of Leominster, Ledbury, Kington and Ross. It was not to be long before he transferred to his father's new milling business—a trade which was to give him much more scope for his creative and inventive flair.

The brewery continued to be the centre of the Imperial empire but eventually Charles decided to diversify and erected a new building on ground to the west of Bewell House. This was St. George's Hall, designed as a roller-skating rink to cater for the demand during one of the earliest crazes for this sport. One wonders how much the father was influenced by the wishes of his children in this enterprise, for it is known that Alfred, at least, became somewhat of an expert. St. George's Hall was a substantial brick building, being some 85 feet long and 65 feet wide, with a gallery and a slate roof. It was one of the first buildings in the city to be lit by electric light and, the bulbs being blue, this caused considerable merriment since the Watkins family were all supporters of the Liberal, Gladstone. When the craze for roller-skating lessened, the building was used for some time as a hall for travelling entertainment companies but, as the expanding brewery required additional room, the hall was taken over to become the hop and ale store.

From 1883 Henry Watkins, by then a partner, managed the whole brewery business until his death shortly after his father, in 1889. The brewery was then managed by two of the other sons, Charles and Alfred. The fourth son, John, had been set up at Pomona Farm, Withington where he specialised in producing apples for the cider trade. With the change-over to the sons, the name reverted to that of the Hereford Brewery. It would appear that neither Alfred nor the younger Charles had any great interest in participating in the daily management of the brewery business, but they were shrewd enough to appoint an excellent manager,

Henry James Hull. Mr. Hull was provided with Bewell House as his residence and was given a reasonably free hand in the running of the whole establishment. By the 1890's the brewery had become the centre of an extensive business. A sales office had been opened in Eign Street (now the bulding which includes the pedestrian passage from Eign Gate to Tesco's) and several hotels, inns and taverns had been bought or leased.

The sales office had frontages to both Eign Street and Bewell Street and presented quite an imposing appearance being three stories high with an ornamental facade including grapes and vines, reflecting the trade of the occupants. In an illustrated booklet *Hereford in 1892*, the main office was described as having 'substantial mahogany fittings, and every convenience is provided for the trans-action of business by the large staff of clerks and others engaged here; the extensive array of ledgers to be seen on the shelves being very suggestive as to the extent and importance of the business transacted.' The upper floors contained suitable private rooms for the use of the manager and the proprietors.

The main buildings of the brewery were arranged on both sides of a private road which led from Bewell Street to Wall Street. The entrance was through an imposing gateway with rusticated stone pillars. On the immediate left on entering were the Brewer's Office and a small warehouse. Next there was a wine and spirit store with cellars underneath. Behind these buildings and fronting onto Bewell Street was the Brewer's House, a reasonably extensive building containing nine main rooms. Edwin Brinkworth was chief brewer to the Watkins and lived here in the 1880's. He was followed by Arthur Baggott who was cellarman at the turn of the century. Behind the Brewer's House was the beer bottling department which had further storage cellars underneath. Immediately to the right of the brewery entry was a shop which belonged to the brewery. In 1898 the shop and premises, containing seven rooms, together with a bakehouse and yard at the rear, and another cottage containing two rooms still further back, were all let on a yearly tenancy to Mr. W.T. Clark, described as a shopkeeper, for £15p.a. They had previ-ously been occupied by Charles Lane who was a basket maker.

The coppers in The Hereford Brewery about 1911

The imposing three-storey brick building with a high, square-sectioned chimney, which stood centrally on the left of the brewery road was the brewhouse, containing the malt room, sugar room, boiler house and engine room. It was here that the malt was crushed and then carried by elevators to the mash-tun where long revolving rakes thoroughly mixed the materials enabling the liquor to extract all the necessary properties from the malt. The liquor was then conducted to the coppers where it was boiled with hops to produce the wort.

The wort was taken through coolers into the large fermentation room, north of the brewhouse, where it was transferred into the fermentation tuns capable of holding some 500 barrels. Yeast was added, and the wort was left until fermentation was complete. The liquor was then drawn off, first into settling tanks and then into store vats. The vat room, on the right of the brewery road, contained huge vats capable of holding many thousands of barrels of ale and stout. Underneath were further extensive cellars used as the ale stores and containing a vast quantity of hogsheads and barrels ready for delivery.

The rear part of the premises included the various buildings where the barrels were cleaned and stored. Here the casks were filled from the store vats and goods were dispatched to their various destinations. Next to the rear gate into Wall Street were the cooper's and wheelwright's shops, for the brewery made and repaired its own casks and wagons. Alongside was a stable with five stalls, a loose box and a harness room. One feels that it was only this rear part of the brewery which had any great attraction to the young Alfred Watkins.

The products of the Hereford Brewery in the latter part of the nineteenth century were many and varied, their names evocative of

An advertisement for the premier brew of The Hereford Brewery in 1892

41

Victorian salesmanship. We should, perhaps, regret the passing of such once famous Hereford brews as Old Household Ale, National Household Pale Ale, Watkins Cream Stout and, most particularly, Golden Sunlight Ale. This latter, which was awarded the only gold medal at the International Exhibition in 1886, was one of their most famous brews. It had a pale golden colour and was likened to the better varieties of German lager beer. In 1892 it was described as being in such great demand, both throughout the kingdom and abroad, that the resources of the brewery were taxed to the very utmost to meet the orders.

By 1892, St. George's Hall had been converted to the production of mineral waters. The Monarch Mineral Water Factory, as it was called, produced what were described as 'the best temperance drinks in existence', many of which, such as Orange Champagne, Lemon Beer and Lemontina, were introduced by the firm.

One of the main reasons given for the success of the brewery in the latter part of the nineteenth century was the quality of the water used in the works. This supply came from the famous Bewell Spring which was on the brewery premises. It was obtained by means of an artesian well, some 40 feet deep, which yielded 'an unfailing supply of excellent brewing liquor'. In fact the well was considerably older than the brewery, for in the early twentieth century Alfred Watkins noted a stone, close to the spring, which read '77ft, Well, 1724'. By 1907 the spring was found to be insufficient for the increased trade. Mr. Chesterman, the local water diviner, was called in and, with no knowledge of the stone, he divined an abundant source some 80 to 90 feet below the surface. A steel pipe was driven and struck a gushing supply at 88 feet deep. The water, which was of crystal clearness and purity and never exceeded 50 degrees Farenheit in temperature, helped to retrieve the brewery's reputation.

The firm acted as their own shippers, importing wines, brandy, rum and gin. They also specialised in whisky, their house brand Glen Melon bidding fair to rival Golden Sunlight in popularity. In 1892 the firm was one of the principal employers in the city and thus had a very important bearing on the commercial wellbeing of the whole area. It gradually amassed a large number of tied houses

HEREFORD.

THE PARTICULARS AND CONDITIONS OF SALE

OF

The Hereford Brewery,

FITTED WITH A

25-QUARTER PLANT,

RESIDENCE AND PREMISES,

AND

50-QUARTER MALTINGS,

HEREFORD,

TOGETHER WITH

35 HOTELS, PUBLIC & BEER HOUSES

AND OTHER PROPERTY,

SITUATE

In the City and Neighbourhood;

ALSO

BRANCHES AT

BIRMINGHAM, CARDIFF & SWANSEA,

AND THE VALUABLE

Trade Marks and Goodwill of the Concern,

WHICH INCLUDES A

CONSIDERABLE TRADE IN WINES AND SPIRITS, BOTTLED BEERS AND MINERAL WATERS.

Which will be Sold by Auction by Messrs.

COLLIER and BOWDICH

At the Auction Mart, Tokenhouse Yard, London,

On MONDAY, the 27th day of JUNE, 1898,

At Two o'clock precisely, in One Lot.

UNLESS PREVIOUSLY DISPOSED OF BY PRIVATE TREATY.

The Property may be viewed, and Particulars (with Plans) obtained of Messrs. GWYNNE JAMES & SON, Solicitors, Hereford ; and of

Messrs. COLLIER & BOWDICH, Brewery Valuers & Auctioneers,
24, Coleman Street, London, E.C.

The introductory page from the sale catalogue of The Hereford Brewery in 1898

throughout the county, thus ensuring its local sales, and dealt with over 200 agencies spread amongst towns and cities throughout the kingdom.

The lack of any great interest in the brewery by the proprietors, Alfred and his brother Charles, came to a head in 1898. The decision was made to sell by auction. By this time the brewing empire was quite large—besides the brewery the sale included 35 hotels, public and beer houses in the city and neighbourhood, and branches in Birmingham, Cardiff and Swansea. With such a large holding the sale had more than a local interest, so it took place in London at the Auction Mart in Tokenhouse Road. Messrs. Collier and Bowditch, brewery valuers and auctioneers of 24 Coleman Street in the City were in charge of the sale and their particulars provide much information. The reason given for the sale was that the joint proprietors were 'desirous of retiring'—at this time Alfred was 43 years old! Much was made of the situation of the brewery, in 'a fine hop and barley growing district' where the raw materials were purchased directly from the farmers.

The total sales of the brewery for the period 1895-7 averaged each year:

Beer (in cask and bottle)	£23,297	7s 0d
Wines, spirits, cider and mineral waters	£11,911	18s 0d
Sundries, including grains and yeasts	£952	5s 0d
Total	£36,160	10s 0d

The fixed plant, which was described in detail, included two 36 horse-power Galloway boilers. One of these had only just been installed, having been made in Manchester in 1897.

The total extent of the brewery and its grounds was nearly one and three-quarter acres, all close to the centre of the city, but the total value of the holding was vastly increased by the number of licenced premises included in the sale. Some, such as the Imperial, the Golden Lion and the Orange Tree, are still well known inns in the city. Others, such as the Grapes and the Three Crowns, have only recently closed their doors, but the remainder are now only a

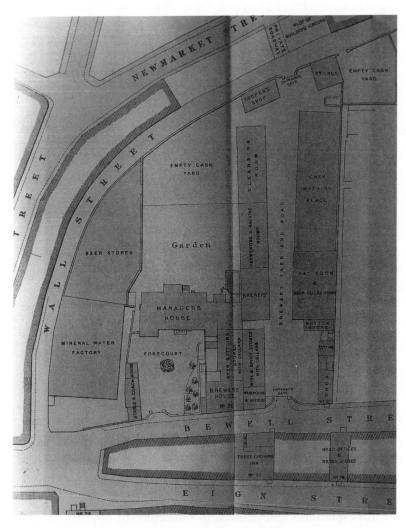

A plan of the brewery as published in the sale catalogue in 1898. Bewell House, the only building which remains, is shown as the manager's house. The mineral water factory was originally St. Georges Hall, a skating rink. Wall Street has since been merged with Edgar Street to form the ring road, the rest of the site being occupied by Tesco's

memory to older Herefordians. The Maidenhead Inn in Eign Street is now Jessons Camping and Clothing Stores; the King's Head in Broad Street was re-built in 1970 but closed a few years later; the Wheatsheaf in Newmarket Street was one of the several inns lost during the construction of the ring road. In Eign Road, on the eastern side of the city, the Barrack Tavern is now a fish and chip shop; and the Whalebone Inn, long the favourite drinking house of bargemen on the River Wye, has lost its upper storey and is now a veterinary surgery. Some were managed houses, but the annual rents for others would be the envy of today's publicans. The highest rent was for the Grapes at £60p.a.; the Orange Tree commanded £30p.a. whilst the poor Whalebone was a mere £18. Several of the houses were in the surrounding villages and five were in Hay (or Hay-on-Wye as it is now known): the King's Head, the Wheatsheaf, the Talbot, the Seven Stars and the Holly Bush.

The Hereford Public Library copy of the sale particulars is annotated in ink with the comment '£64,000 highest bid for the lot'. The business was sold to The Tredegar Brewery Company which then became known as The Hereford and Tredegar Brewery Ltd. With this merger, the interests of Alfred Watkins in the fate of the brewery was at an end, but its story is worthy of completion.

In 1906, the brewery was extended and modernised when the group's breweries at Tredegar and Brecon were closed. It was to continue to produce beers 'from wholesome and edible agricultural products' for many years. At various times in its later life it was part of The Hereford and Cardiff Brewery, The Cheltenham and Hereford Brewery, West Country Breweries and eventually, Whitbreads. The Hereford Brewery was considered large in the latter years of the nineteenth century, but the series of amalgamations and takeovers, which were to culminate in the few large brewing firms we have at present, had their inevitable result; Hereford was relegated to becoming a bottling plant, and eventually, as further economies were made, it was closed.

All the buildings which had comprised the brewery itself were demolished by the early 1960's, the cellars filled with rubble and the whole area then turned into a car park. Various developments were

The brewery in the early twentieth century, showing the third floor extension onto the brewhouse

suggested for this prime area of the city but all were rejected. It was not until 1981, when the large area to the east (which had become a jam factory after the demolition of the slum housing) also became available, that a scheme to build a large supermarket for Tesco's was accepted. The large collection of empty bottles, which were retrieved by archaeologists from the infilled cellars as they were cleared, remain as a mute testimony to the efforts and endeavours of the Watkins family and the later brewers who, between them, occupied the site for almost a hundred years.

The only building to survive the wholesale demolition was Bewell House—the one building which pre-dated the brewery, and the only one considered to be of sufficient architectural importance to merit its renovation and re-use for offices.

Small, local breweries are coming into existence once more and several pubs are now making their own brews. Although we will never again be able to savour the pleasant flavour of Golden Sunlight Ale and the mellowness of Glen Melon whisky as produced at the Hereford Brewery, we are once again able to appreciate beers with the proud label 'Made in Hereford'.

*Some of the bottles used by Watkins' Hereford Brewery
and found during the excavations for the Tesco supermarket in 1982*

III

The Flour Mills

The Hereford Foundry in Friars Street had been built by Captain Radford in 1834. As a foundry it does not appear to have been very successful and it was taken over by Alfred's father, Charles Watkins, in about 1876. He adapted some of the existing buildings and extended them and they then became the Imperial Flour Mills and associated maltings.

Alfred Watkins had been working as a traveller for the brewery but, finding that business rather uncongenial, he transferred to the new business, continuing to travel around the Herefordshire countryside, but visiting all the out-lying farmers rather than back-street inns.

The flour mills were still making use of the traditional mill stones operated by steam power for grinding the grain. This was a laborious and time-consuming operation in a dark and gloomy factory building, probably lit by gas. Within a year of his father taking over the business, the young Watkins had introduced a dynamo into the building—the first in the whole of the county—thus enabling the works to be lit by electricity. This would not just have been a factory improvement, it would have created a tremendous impression throughout the city, demonstrating the modern nature of the mill. It would also have provided the impetus for the eventual introduction of electric light throughout the city.

But Watkins was not content with this innovation—he wanted to ensure that the mill was the most efficient in the county. By 1882, he decided that the old grinding stones had to go and be replaced with

The Imperial Flour Mill early in the twentieth century. The building on the left was the original foundry. For many years there was a spur off the main railway line from Barton Station to the mill

a roller milling plant, which he planned and erected. But his interest spread to all corners of the business, for he was studying every aspect of milling during these early years and in 1883 he won the premier silver medal in the City and Guilds examination.

By the time of Charles Watkins' death in 1888, the importance of the combined brewery and flour mill in the life of the city can be gained from his obituary. 'From the time of taking over the flour mills to the present date these undertakings have progressed in a wonderful degree, and have enabled the late proprietor, for a considerable number of years, to be a great employer of labour.'

Of course there are many different types of flour, each of which can be used to produce a different type of bread. One critical factor is the proportion of the roughage left with the wheat flour. This roughage, often praised by dieticians, is in fact the indigestible wheat offal which tends to make bread rather gritty and, to some people, unpleasant. Watkins must have done many experiments until, in the 1890's, he perfected a flour which he considered to produce a brown loaf with an ideal spongy, honeycomb structure. The flour contained no offal but included a balanced proportion of the germ of the wheat—it was not a wholemeal as we understand it today. This he called Vagos, as the flour was milled in the Wye valley, and the Roman name for the river was Vaga, meaning 'The Wandering Maiden'.

The test of any bread is, of course, in its looks and taste, and the texture and slightly malted flavour of bread made from Vagos flour meant it became very popular with local shops. But this was not sufficent for Watkins and he began to explore the possibilities of nationwide sales for his flour.

During the latter part of the nineteenth century, bakers, with their special breads, and millers, with their secret recipes for flour, used to hold an annual nationwide Bakers Exhibition at the

The grinding stones in the flour mill at about the turn of the century

51

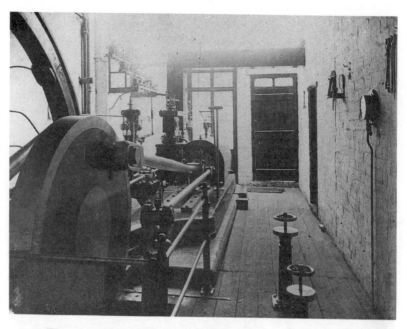

The engine house at the flour mill about the turn of the century

Agricultural Hall in Islington. With sales of Vagos flour increasing throughout the country, the firm, which by then had Watkins and his elder brother Charles as partners, decided to take a stand. As part of the exhibition they then instituted an annual competition with a cash prize, open to all Vagos bakers. Watkins' son, Allen accompanied his father on several trips to London for these exhibitions and recollects the loaves, all cut in half to expose the texture, being judged for quality by bread experts.

The London visits, at the turn of the century, must have been full of excitement for a youngster from one of the more remote country towns. In his biography of his father, Allen recalled that:

'His senior help was a jovial fellow from Hereford whose name was Jackson. It was pretty hard work for a boy of eleven: twelve hours a day, 8 a.m. to 8 p.m. We had to stagger our meals, and once or twice I was left in sole charge. There was not a lot to do, but it could be embarrassing if close enquiries were made. However, I was

Alfred Watkins in his late 20's (Bennett & Son, Worcester)

briefed in the main outlines, and soon learned how to dodge the awkward question.

'At the end of the week I would be tired out, but loved it all—the cobbled roadway of Upper Street, the market stalls, the chop-house (complete with sawdust and spittoons) where father drank lager and I ginger beer with our chops, the steamer up to Hampton Court on the Sunday—it was an exciting new world.'

Alfred Watkins' elder brother retired from active participation in the mill's affairs early in the twentieth century. At this time Watkins had many other interests and was not prepared to be a full-time managing director at the mill. He decided to take on a partner who would be responsible for the day-to-day running of the establishment. This was E.S. Newman who was an exceptionally able miller, interested and capable in increasing efficiency and making the works profitable. The Vagos bread was only a small part of the mill's output and, under Newman's efficiency drive, its sales were allowed to dwindle and finally cease completely.

After Watkins' death his son Allen, who then lived in Cheam, continued in partnership with Newman but only visited occasionally whilst Newman worked at the mill seven days a week. Eventually Allen Watkins sold his majority shareholding to Newman, retaining only a minority holding. A new company, Watkins Flour Mills Ltd., was formed with three directors—Newman, Watkins and Arthur Russell who had become the manager, although firm control was retained by Newman.

In the long term, the loss of Vagos may well have been a mistake. Many years later Russell said to Allen 'You know, it was a tragedy for you that Vagos was given up. Your father would have made his fortune if the firm had been allowed to go on with it.'

At that time the secret formula was still known for it had been kept by Arthur Cruse, who had been a clerk in the firm for over fifty years. Russell may well have started up production again but it was not to be—he died suddenly of heart failure, and the last chance was gone.

Another of Watkins' enterprises, The Watkins Meter Company, was in a building attached to the flour mills and, apart from making

Loading the steam wagon at the Watkins' Imperial Flour Mills
(Alfred Watkins, 1905)

photographic meters of various types, also made some equipment associated with the baking of bread. The patented Baker's Thermometer was essentially a simple thermometer but with a second scale which established the necessary heat of the liquor (for making up the dough) having first found the temperature of the flour. The calculation made on the scale of the instrument was, according to the instructions, 'based on a two year's series of trials in an average bakehouse.'

A second piece of apparatus was much more complex and was an excellent example of Watkins' inventive flair. This was the dough-meter, brought out in two different patented forms—the bell doughmeter and the more-refined clock doughmeter. Its purpose was to establish the correct length of time between starting the yeast and putting the bread in the oven. This was something that the baker had done previously only by experience. Watkins, as he also did in the photographic fields of exposure and development, aimed to put this on a scientific footing. In the instructions he said 'The doughmeter does not supersede the baker's experience, but gives him a new and accurate power of gauging when his fermentation has attained just the result suited to his trade. It is to dough-making what a speedometer is to a motor car driver.'

The method used in the doughmeter was to measure accurately the time that it took for the dough to expand by exactly 25 per cent of its original size. The basic part of the machine was a dough-holder which contained 1lb 14 ozs of dough. On top of this (in the refined version) was placed the clock, which had been set going when the yeast was started (mixing with flour and liquor). When the dough had expanded by the required 25 per cent, a trigger was activated which stopped the clock (in the earlier version it rang a bell). The clock recorded what Watkins called the meter time. To determine the total time from starting the yeast to putting the dough in the oven, this meter time had to be multiplied by a factor which varied betwen two and three-quarters (for a very weak flour) to four (with the strongest possible flour). A normal factor, for blended flour, was about three and was dependent on how far the baker wanted to carry his fermentation to secure the loaf best suited to his trade. The total time was taken off the bakehouse clock.

The doughmeter came complete with the clock, a disc type calculator, a time board and a baker's note book (the latter for keeping a permanent record). When it was first produced it was described as 'an entirely new instrument which follows an entirely new method'. Was this one of the reasons for the success of the Vagos bread?

Watkins continued to have an active interest in the flour mill for the whole of his life. Even in 1927, when he was in his early 70's, he commented that he was still occasionally 'on the road' making trade journeys.

IV

The Bee Meter Company

In this age of the fully automatic camera where all the user needs to do is point his pocket-sized machine at the subject and press a button, we tend to forget the complexities and difficulties which had to be overcome to take a successful photograph during the latter part of the nineteenth century. Alfred Watkins remembered this in the introduction to his book *Photography: its Principles and Applications* written in 1911 when he said:

'I write this in a Radnorshire roadside inn; the landlady comes in with the bedroom candle; and I bring to mind the day thirty-five years ago when she first came to the inn, for I called on her that very day. It was on a business-driving journey, and in the trap was my wet plate photographic kit. What a proceeding it was in those days; the pitching of the portable tent, sitting on one's heels inside, drawing the flaps, coating the plate with collodion, dipping it in the silver bath to sensitise, carrying out to expose, not far away, for it must be developed while still wet, again cramped, within the low tent. And yet with all the obstacles difficult subjects were attempted. Over the other side of that great mountain mass—the Radnor Forest—I remember turning out one cold winter's morning and taking scenes on the little frozen stream with the trees hung with hoar frost, and a lighted spirit lamp required in the tent to thaw needles of ice in bath and developer. Those were simple days, when lantern slides and negatives of moving subjects were alike made on one sensitive film—wet collodion—and varying "speeds of plates" were almost unknown.'

Watkins' camera and carrying case in Hereford City Museum
(Ken Hoverd, 1990)

This must have been during 1876 when Watkins was about 21. At that time he suffered from the problem which beset all early photographers—calculating the length of exposure needed for a successful photograph. Standard exposure tables, depending upon season, latitude, time of day and weather conditions were complex and highly inaccurate. The alternative was trial and error—expensive in materials and wasteful in time. Watkins was one of the first people to appreciate that the main prerequisites of a good photograph was not the choice of camera, lens or plate, but the correct determination of both exposure and development times.

The first problem he tackled was that of exposure; the requirement was a method of measuring the relative intensity of light. Watkins resolved this by inventing the actinometer, which measured the intensity of the ambient light by counting the number of seconds that it took for a piece of sensitized paper to darken to the same tint as a fixed reference paper. This, together with a knowledge of the size of the aperture or diaphragm of the camera and the speed of the plate used are the three factors which affect exposure. The aperture and the plate speed could be reduced to numerical values and the actinometer now produced a numerical value for the light.

The problem of exposure was solved and Watkins proceeded to design and make what was, in effect, a pocket calculator for determining exposure. This, the first exposure meter, consisted of an actinometer with revolving scales for the other two factors. The invention was patented and a paper on the subject was published in the *British Journal of Photography* in April 1890.

Although it was described as being merely ingenious and commercially of little use, Watkins was convinced that his invention would allow any photographer, however inexperienced, to produce a correctly exposed photograph. He decided to set up his own business to manufacture and sell his exposure meters and started operations in a small workroom adjoining the Imperial Flour Mills. This building, which still stands, was always simply known as The Meter Works. In the first year of production he sold 1,400 meters at a guinea each. The business was successful and he soon produced a

A selection of Watkins' exposure meters and instruction booklets in Hereford City Museum (Ken Hoverd, 1990)

popular version—the famous Bee Meter (a name selected to suggest something small and highly efficient) which, in its various forms, became the standard addition to every photographer's kit for almost half a century.

One question which was raised many times was—would the Watkins meter work in other parts of the world where the light was of a different quality? Its total success was finally demonstrated to all when H.G. Ponting, the photographer who accompanied Scott's Antarctic Expedition in 1910, used a Watkins meter to produce his amazing landscapes of this, at the time almost totally unknown, southern continent. On his return he wrote to Watkins to tell him that without the meter the work would have been impossible.

Following on from this impeccable reference, sales rapidly grew and became world-wide; instructions for the use of the meter were produced in most European languages. An order was even received from China—a meter was sent and the requisite half-crown was eventually received. Allen Watkins records this event as one of his father's most treasured experiences.

The meter was remembered for years after Watkins' death for in 1940 Turner wrote in his book *Photographic Exposure* 'As far as the author knows the first meter of any kind (as distinct from calculators) was the Watkins put on the market about 1890 and continuing in manufacture till Mr. Watkins died in 1935. It will not, we think, be out of place to say a word or two in honour of Watkins who was one of the first to realise fully the implications of the work of Hurter and Driffield. The fundamental point on which those pioneers insisted, was the necessity for correct exposure, and further that errors in exposure could not be corrected by special measures in development.'

The second basic problem that had to be resolved was that of development and Watkins was determined to solve this by establishing a quantitive method which would produce precise results. His *Factorial Method of Development* was published in 1894. It was based on his own experiments and made use of what became known as the Watkins Factor. He established that to get a standard degree of contrast it was necessary to measure the time that it took from

Watkins Bee Meter advertisement (Alfred Watkins)

pouring the developer on the plate to the first appearance of any trace of the image. Multiplying this time by the factor would then give the precise development time required for perfect results. The factor, of course, varied with the developer and Watkins carried out many experiments to establish the correct figures to use in each case. The Watkins Meter Company eventually produced a dark-room clock and a factorial calculator to aid photographers in obtaining the correct development times.

Most of Watkins' experiments in development were carried out in his dark room in the cellar of Vineyard Croft. He did not rely on expensive equipment but made use of whatever came to hand. His son, who was brought up at Vineyard Croft, described the cellar steps as a death-trap with the steepest treads he had ever seen. Apart from the dark room, the rest of the cellar was full of shelves of apples which came from the large garden!

In 1894 Watkins was elected a Member of the Royal Photographic Society; in 1910 he became a Fellow and in the same year he received their coveted Progress Medal for his extensive researches into photographic theory and practice. Only ten such medals had previously been issued and, at the presentation, the president, Lord Crawford, said 'the mere fact of the society giving the highest honour at its command to Mr. Watkins this year stamps his methods and inventions with a significance which no other society in the world could give to them.'

Watkins' first camera was a cigar box with a pinhole for the lens, and he remained attached to this simple mehod of photography throughout his life, eventually marketing special pinhole lenses through the meter company. These had several sizes of pinhole and could be attached to ordinary cameras as a substitute for the glass

A Watkins darkroom clock made at The Meter Works and a simple pinhole camera, both in Hereford City Museum (Ken Hoverd, 1990)

lens. Such a camera has the advantage that it can work at any focus, can be used for wide or narrow angle views and gives an artistic texture to the photograph. The main disadvantage is in the length of time needed for the exposure which was, with the slow plates then available, measured in minutes rather than seconds. A further disadvantage, using the standard camera body of the period, was that the image could only be seen on the focussing screen in very bright light. This problem Watkins solved with typical simplicity—'having levelled the stand and noted that the pinhole is opposite the centre of the plate, turn the camera round, and lifting the focussing screen apply the eye to the pinhole and see if the view wanted is framed in the end of the camera. Then turn the camera round again for the pinhole to face the subject.'

For those who consider making such a camera, Watkins advises 'a 100-cigar box, flor-fina size, which will take a quarter plate. The box can be made light-tight by wrapping it in two thicknesses of black cloth. The box can then be placed on some firm support to take the photograph and weighted down with a stone.' This description is included in Watkins' first book on photography *The Watkins Manual of Exposure and Development*, published in 1894 jointly by Simkin Marshall Ltd. and the Watkins Meter Company. It was followed by ten further editions, each revised by the author.

The first section of the book was designed for complete beginners—how to start and what to buy, and how to take and process photographs. Watkins explains his own choice of camera, namely one taking a plate size of seven and a half inches by five inches, similar in proportion to the present A5 sheet of paper and was wider than the then standard half-plate. He considered it to be more useful for landscapes than for portraits. It is evident both from this and from his complete collection of negatives in Hereford City Library that Watkins had little or no interest in portrait work. He also comments that his choice of camera 'is practically the largest size that a man of average strength can carry on a long day's tramp.'

The main part of the book deals with exposure and development where Watkins shows his considerable expertise and his ability to explain the technicalities of the subject in simple language. So, for example, in discussing when to stop development he compares the problem to a railway journey where 'it does not matter whether you travel by goods or express, so long as you get out at the right station.'

The final section is just labelled Jottings and shows Watkins both as a practical man and as an improviser. It contains snippets of practical advice such as 'fish glue is indispensible for all kinds of repairs' (to photographic prints); 'a modern shape of ale glass used by publicans is just the thing for dark-room use—they may be marked at the 2oz and 4oz level with a file, the marks being filled in with brunswick black' and 'a cheap print washer can be made out of a lard bucket'.

At the rear of the book is a price list of the various photographic aids made by the the company—the 1911 edition lists the standard Bee Meter at 2 shillings and 6 pence whilst the top of the range chronograph and meter combined cost 35 shillings. By comparison the 141 page Watkins manual sold for 1 shilling.

Watkins was also writing regular articles on photography for various journals. Two, published in successive issues of *The Field Naturalists Quarterly* during 1902, show the breadth of his researches. The first was called *Animal Photography* in which he described the best type of equipment and methods, and there were typically practical hints from a master of improvisation. Thus, if you wanted to photograph a toad or frog 'put a box over the top of it on a previously focussed spot. Allow it to settle and then raise the box and expose.' The second article discussed methods applicable to *Record Photography*, and included many more practical comments.

A comprehensive work on photography was lacking in the early twentieth century, and so in 1910 Constable and Co. asked Watkins if he would be prepared to write one. *Photography: its Principles and Applications* was published in 1911 and rapidly became the standard reference book, even containing a chapter on colour photography, the coloured frontispiece being a garden scene taken from an autochrome by Watkins. This process, invented by Lumiére of Lyons, had only been issued commercially in 1907 so was still very new and exciting. A review of the book, published in *The Morning Post*, concluded that 'There are few photographers of experience who will not be of opinion that the conclusions and experiences of Mr. Watkins are worth a library of compiled text-books.'

Watkins also took an early interest in the cinema and went to Chester in 1890 to see a demonstration by Mr. Friese Green, the inventor of the cine projector and the first person to take and produce a series of negatives on a continuous band of celluloid film. This, the first moving film picture ever produced, featured a human hand opening and shutting. Watkins himself, later on, possessed a hand-turned cine camera, and some 35mm films made by him of events in Hereford survive and are now stored in the archives of the British Film Institute. These films include Kitchener's recruits marching past the Hereford Eye Hospital in 1914, and some of the first motorcycle trials which took place on Stockley Hill.

The Watkins Meter Company, operating from the small shed-like building next to the Imperial Flour Mill in Friar Street, may well have been of greater interest and thus more important to Watkins than his major business enterprise. It operated with a staff of four, the manager Mr. McKaig and three young men who operated the

The interior of The Meter Works during the First World War
when it was used for light industrial purposes

lathes and put the instruments together. Watkins personally dealt with all the correspondence from other photographers and must have been responsible for most of the experimental work and the improved designs of specialist light meters, daylight developing tanks, thermometers, dark-room clocks and other equipment. During the First World War the company works was used for light engineering, but once the war was over Watkins went back to producing photographic equipment and the business continued successfully until his death.

In his will Watkins left the works to his manager Mr. McKaig, who had always been a close friend. But shortly after Watkins' own death, Mckaig fell seriously ill and after considerable suffering died of cancer. McKaig's young nephew, who in turn succeeded to the company, was not capable of dealing with the problems associated with the business and, becoming depressed, hanged himself in the works building. It was a most unfortunate end to what had been an innovative and important business which, for many years, had helped photographers throughout the world.

For some time afterwards the Bee Meter business continued to be handled by Godfrey Davies, a friend and colleague of Watkins, from his Wye Val Photographic Shop in Broad Street, Hereford, where he produced refills for the meter until demand gradually ceased around the beginning of the Second World War.

Apart from being an innovator of the first order, Watkins also promoted photography and the photographer in other ways. In November 1895 he, together with some of his friends, founded The Herefordshire Photographic Society, one of the first such societies in the country. It met occasionally to exchange information and study photographic techniques. At this time Watkins was some thirty years old and in addition to his photographic interests must have been courting his wife-to-be, for he married the following year.

The first president of the newly formed society was James Rankin M.P., later to be knighted, and meetings were held at Clarence House in Aubrey Street in the city. In 1892 Alderman Blake of Ross was elected president and the society started to hold field meetings during the summer months as well as indoor events in the winter.

Thus, in 1894, members went on a boating trip down the Wye from Ross to Monmouth, presumably taking all their heavy photographic equipment and tripods with them.

In 1898 the society held its first public exhibition of members' work in the public library in Broad Street and following this, membership gradually increased to about one hundred. Ladies were allowed to join the society and, in a second exhibition during 1899, there was even a ladies competition. (It is interesting to note the differing attitude to the membership of ladies in the rather technical Photographic Society as compared with that in the more academic Woolhope Club, where lady membership was strongly opposed for many years.) As part of this event, several lectures were given and Watkins showed his considerable knowledge and expertise by talking on colour photography—at that time a very complex and time-consuming process. The exhibition continued this theme by including several examples of his early colour photographs.

By 1900 Watkins was one of the vice-presidents of the society which, in 1906, moved to new rooms at 76 Eign Street where they

Detail from a photograph of the Photographic Convention of the U.K. meeting at Hereford in 1907, showing Alfred Watkins (seated, fourth from left)

remained until 1914. It was in 1907 that the twenty-second annual meeting of the Photographic Convention of the United Kingdom was held in Hereford, as a mark of respect for Watkins who was president of the convention for that year. About eighty delegates from all over the country attended the six day meeting and Watkins gave the inaugural address. Delegates were greeted by members of a reception committee which included many of the most illustrious figures in the county including the mayor, Cllr. G.C. Caldwell; the Lord Lieutenant, Sir John Cotterell; the dean, the Hon. and Very Rev. J.W. Leigh; Lord Biddulph; Sir James Rankin; Sir John Arkwright, then president of the Hereford society, and many others. In the evening, after the official reception, there was a musical promenade and a display of the city charters and plate. The following week was full of excursions to local beauty spots including Weobley, Pembridge, Ledbury, Abbey Dore, Kilpeck and Bosbury. As president of the convention, Watkins and his wife held an 'At Home' at Vineyard Croft for all the delegates. Apart from the usual hospitality, the Watkins also offered their visitors boating and punting on the Wye!

The programme booklet contained several articles of local interest including one by Watkins on Hereford in which he described some of the historic buildings that delegates would visit during their stay. Other articles included one by the dean entitled *Notes on Hereford Cathedral* and one by Ella Mary Leather (who five years later was to have her book *Folklore of Herefordshire* published by Jakeman and Carver of Hereford) about the villages of Weobley and Pembridge.

In 1907 Walter Pilley, a friend of Watkins, was elected president of the society, a position he held until about 1912 when he was succeeded by Watkins himself. It was during this year that the first lady, Miss Gladstone, was elected to the council of the society.

Although meetings continued to be held during the First World War this was obviously a dificult period, and membership gradually dropped to about twenty. It is evident that Watkins was not satisfied with the general affairs of the society and in 1921 he wrote to the council apologising for his non-attendance at their meeting due to illness and resigned as president. He said that he was willing to continue as a member and do what he could in the interests of the society 'providing the society was completely reorganised'.

This was apparently agreed to and Sir John Arkwright was elected president with Godfrey Davies acting as both secretary and treasurer. At that time Davies was the youngest member of the society, and indeed had only joined in 1919. The society was also in debt and several fund-raising efforts were held. The 1920's continued to be difficult years and the society again suffered from falling numbers. It eventually folded and all activities were suspended in 1927.

Watkins was never to know that the society which he had helped to form was to be reborn in 1937 some two years after his death. Despite the Second World War, membership increased steadily and contrary to all expectations this became one of the most successful periods in the whole of the society's history. In 1943, when wartime restrictions were at their peak, it was decided that the society would arrange a series of lectures to be called The Alfred Watkins Memorial Lectures with the objects of 'keeping alive the memory of that pioneer worker and of encouraging still further development of photography in every sphere.'

The inaugural lecture, held in the town hall on 23 July 1943, was given by F.J. Mortimer, who had been editor of *The Amateur Photographer* for almost forty years. His subject was topical—Photography's Part in the War—and attracted an audience of some 400 people. During the lecture he disclosed that film processing in the R.A.F. was carried out entirely by the time and temperature method invented by Watkins.

The second memorial lecture was held later in the same year, on 14 October. It was given by Donald McMaster, the managing director of the British division of Kodak and president of the Royal Photographic Society. His subject, The Next Decade in Photography, forecast the appearance of cheap, small cameras with synchronised flash—effectively the sort of cameras which are used by most people today. After his lecture Mr. McMaster opened the first Anglo-American Salon of Photography in the city library which drew over 1,000 visitors. When, some time later, Mr. McMaster returned to America in overall charge of Kodak, he was responsible for the addition of a separate section devoted to the inventions of Watkins at their museum of photography, at George Eastman House in New York.

To Watkins, photography had always been a technical subject in which the operator had to have a wide knowledge of the background principles in order to produce a quality picture. This did not mean that he must have expensive equipment—Watkins himself was the great improviser—but rather that he must understand the techniques and latest developments in what was then a scientific field of study for everyone who participated.

This was well illustrated in the tale his son told of his father sending a set of mounted photographs of a local estate to its owner. In his letter of thanks the owner made the rather unfortunate comment 'What a splendid camera you must have Mr. Watkins!' Some time later the owner sent Watkins a brace of pheasants; 'What a splendid gun you must have, Sir John!' rejoined Watkins.

Watkins was not just a technical expert, he also had a true sense of composition. His son, Allen, could not have put it better when he said of his father 'his love of Herefordshire came out in his photographs.' Allen emphasised this in a letter to the Hereford Times shortly after the centenary of his father's birth when he wrote 'Driving his steam car he would stop suddenly in the middle of nowhere and exclaim "Just look at that group of Hereford cows with the old stone bridge over the brook in the foreground: what a picture. I must get a negative of that at once. The evening side-light will be just right." And out would come his camera.'

During his later life it would appear that he was becoming somewhat disillusioned for in 1927 he wrote 'I see a slackening rate in real advance and a poorer public standard in results, coinciding with the decay of the amateur craftsman—a public quite indifferent to photographic knowledge.'

One wonders what Watkins would think of the standards of photography at the present day where the operator with his small but fully automatic and self-winding camera merely points it at the subject and presses a button.

V

Historic Hereford

'Alfred Watkins loved his native city and had its interest ever at heart'. So wrote George Marshall in the long obituary published in the Hereford Times on Saturday 13 April 1935. It was this affection, coupled with the regular use of his camera to record the changes which were taking place in the city down to the most minute detail, which made him one of the most important observers of his period. Although he regularly examined excavations and trenches in the city he was seldom involved in formal archaeological work, being content to watch and record the efforts of others. He also examined historic buildings, especially if they were under threat, and although he did not produce many formal drawings, he described and photographed them and thus produced a record which is still of considerable use today. He combined the rare ability, which is always the trademark of the great archaeologist, of being able to interpret the complexities of buildings, trench sections, and other man-made features, with a capacity to enthrall an audience with his findings.

We will never be sure what it was that gave the young Watkins his absorbing interest in the past history of his home town. It is evident, from the occasional comment in his published works that this interest was present at a very early age, although it was not apparently something which he obtained from his parents and was patently not a result of his education at the private school run by the Reverend Bowell.

One of the earliest of his childhood memories must have been the demolition of the Market Hall in High Town in 1862 when he

*The Market Hall in High Town, Hereford,
shortly before it was demolished in 1862*

was barely seven. He mentions the 'dim but vivid memory of the
clustered columns' in his guide to the Old House published in
1934. In its time the Market Hall was one of the most important and
impressive buildings in the whole of the county. It was thirty-five feet
wide and eighty-five feet long standing on a raised, stone-flagged
floor two steps high. When it was built in the latter part of the
sixteenth century it was three stories high, standing on twenty-seven
wooden columns with an open ground floor for the market. On the
first floor were the magistrates chambers and the assize court, with
the city guilds (fourteen in all including bakers, barbers, butchers,
clothiers, coopers, glovers, tanners and weavers) on the second
floor. At the end of the eighteenth century the top floor was
deemed unsafe and the building was reduced to a two storey edifice.
This was then stuccoed, thus losing much of its elevational splen-
dour, and although plans were prepared for its restoration these
came to nought and the building was finally demolished—being
sold to William Davies of Widemarsh Street for £200. Its position
and size can still be appreciated by the visitor to High Town, for the

Posts and spandrels belonging to Hereford's Market Hall, re-erected as an aviary, itself to become the summer-house pictured at Holmer Park (Alfred Watkins)

places where the twenty-seven pillars once stood are marked out with coloured paving stones.

Watkins would probably have discovered more about this building as a teenager for some of the major parts of the structure, including four pillars and several decorated spandrels, were re-used to make an aviary in the grounds of Holmer Park. It can still be seen on the side of the minor road leading eastwards off the A49 at the rear of Holmer Park, itself now Inco-Alloys' social club.

The young Watkins grew up in a city which was in the throes of Victorian expansion. As the population increased and became more prosperous, new houses were built in what had been open country-side. In the centre of the city many half-timbered buildings were being 'modernised' with new brick facades, whilst others were totally demolished and rebuilt. The railways did not arrive in Hereford until 1854, the year before Alfred Watkins was born, and further lines were added when he was young. He remembered this when he was discussing the source of a spring which runs into the Wye next to the Hunderton railway bridge (now only used by pedestrians and cyclists). He explained from his personal observations that 'This was caused by the cutting of the Newport Railway near the Moorfields breaking into a copious land spring, which had to be piped to the Wye. It lowered all the city wells a foot at that time. Hereford is full of disused wells, going down sixteen or eighteen feet into the water-bearing gravel beds.'

Another childhood memory, involving one of the most historic sites in the city, emerges in an article written in 1933 when he was then 78 years old. In the article he discusses the possibility of an underground passage, possibly associated with Hereford Castle, which was reputed to have been visible in the late nineteenth century close to where the Victoria suspension bridge was built in 1898. He demonstrates that this supposed passage was a culvert— the old outlet for the stream which fed the castle mill. He then goes on to say 'My knowledge of the spot goes further back to my child-hood of scrambling down the then gully here and over the ruined walls and foundations of the ancient castle mill then being demolished. This must have been about 1861. It was in 1863 that I heard

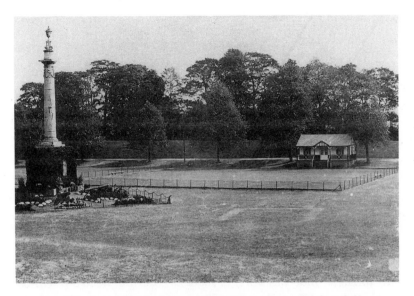

*Parch marks on Castle Green which indicate the buried foundations
of long-lost buildings (Alfred Watkins, 1933)*

the Russian gun fired on the marriage of the Princess Alexandria,
being present on Castle Green, and remember running off behind
Hogg's Mount to escape the terrible hurt of the drums of my young
ears, for the concussion broke many windows at the hospital. The
site of the castle mill was not that of the hospital lodge, as usually
stated, but low down in the trough of the stream running from the
mill pool or moat, as clearly shown on Speede's map.'

From this it is apparent that Alfred was scrambling about the
castle mill ruins, close by the river bank, at the tender age of six. His
memory of these early events never deserted him and some seventy
years later he was still able to provide vivid images of the things seen
as a child.

There have often been suggestions that there are secret passages
underneath Castle Green and when I was supervising an archaeological excavation there in 1971 I was approached by a local diviner
for permission to examine the area. I agreed and some time later,
when he was packing up the tools of his trade, I asked him what he

had discovered. He assured me that there were several tunnels underneath the green and that they were all about thirty feet below the surface. When he told me that one of the tunnels was full of gold and silver, I decided that this was all within the realms of fantasy and went back to the problems of excavating the Saxon cemetery which was in use before the castle was built.

Several years later, when checking some obscure documentary references, I came across a comment by Walter Pilley, who was a notable local antiquary during the nineteenth century. He was present when a sewer was being laid at a depth of between thirty and forty feet across the green in 1886. 'At the bottom of the manhole (at the west end of Castle Green) on the south side, was a subterranean passage built of stone. The arch of the passage was about six feet high by about four feet wide. In the passage were seen two or three skeletons, also a pitcher jug in perfect condition. Unfortunately while the workman was lifting it up, a mass of earth fell, breaking it all to pieces. Close to this was a deep well, (with) walls lined with stone.'

Castle Green, originally the city cemetery surrounding the monastery of St. Guthlac's, later became the site of the royal fortress which, according to Leland who visited Hereford on his travels early in the sixteenth century, was 'one of the fayrest, largest, and strongest castels in England' being 'in circuit nearly as large as that of Windsor'. For that there is evidence, but it would appear the green may still contain the deeply buried evidence of a significant and totally unknown event in the turbulent past of this historic city.

Much later in his life Watkins recorded several burials unearthed during drainage works, thus providing the basic framework for later archaeologists working on the Saxon cemetery whilst he also observed further traces of the castle. 'The opportunity came with the long drought of 1933, when the sun of our glorious summer had bleached in patches the turf on the Castle Green, as if on a stony hillside, leaving between the green of normal pasture. In places, straight lines of whitened grass of even width appeared, with other lines at right angles, forming in at least three cases (which I roughly surveyed and measured up) the outlines of foundations of rectilinear buildings, twenty to twenty-seven feet in length, and with walls two to four feet thick. Beside these were two long lines of similar marks, probably boundary walls, although a suggestion has been made that they mark the line of underground passages.'

Watkins considered one of the buildings to be a tower and the other a chapel but was never to see his theories proved. However, in 1960, small trial excavations by F.G. Heys on the latter site confirmed the accuracy of the twenty-seven year old theory, exposing parts of the nave and chancel. The traces of buried foundations can still be seen as long parched marks in the grass whenever there is a dry summer. They relate to some of the many buildings which once stood on Castle Green and which, according to an inventory of 1265, included three halls: the king's great hall, the king's small hall, and the county hall. There were also chambers for the king and queen and their knights, an almonry, a counting house, a stable, two gaols, a chamber for the king's clerks, an exchequer chamber, a building in which siege engines were kept and the usual offices (kitchen, bakery and so forth).

If the postulated subterranean passages at the castle were impossible to prove, there were still others to ponder. One, often mentioned in contemporary literature, was carefully investigated by Watkins. This passage was supposed to run from St. Guthlac's Priory in Commercial Road where the bus station now stands, to the Vineyard, a small area once owned by the monks and which eventually became a parish in its own right. In commenting on this supposed passage, Watkins' opening paragraph typified his scientific approach when he wrote 'I propose to bring together whatever records I can find of actual personal observation of this supposed passage near the Vineyard. In doing so I shall try to separate the theories and perhaps traditions which are almost invariably given at the time of recording any observation of fact, and which only too often are mere guesses.'

He goes on to describe the various records of the feature, continues with an outline of the many suggestions which had previously been propounded and, almost disappointingly, comes to the conclusion that all the cavities seen were due to natural causes.

Many people in the city are still of the opinion that there is a passage which starts under the city-side arch of the Wye Bridge. Watkins must have discussed this with Harry Jordan, who had a boatyard on the opposite side of the river, for he wrote, in a letter to the Hereford Times, 'Harry Jordan once told me that he had crawled up it as far as opposite the Black Lion, and that it apparently turned down for Gwynne Street. It is an old sewer, probably not very old.'

He finishes his letter with the comment 'The only evidence I know for one (subterranean tunnel) in this county is a short passage through the King's Ditch, which connects a cellar under the Booth Hall with one against East Street.'

Although the gates leading into the city had been demolished over fifty years before he was born, many stretches of the city wall still survived and he recorded and photographed several sections which have since disappeared. About 1898 he hurried to the corner of Widemarsh Street and Newmarket Street to photograph a section of the old wall, which included a fifteenth century postern gate,

The city wall near the site of Widemarsh Gate being demolished
to make way for the new Wellington Inn (Alfred Watkins, c.1898)

The city wall, since demolished, at the western end of West Street in 1903.
The smooth clay exposed in the lower part of the bank behind the wall is the
first recognised unearthing of the Saxon defences (Alfred Watkins)

exposed after the old Wellington Inn had been pulled down. The
photograph shows the workmen demolishing what was, very obviously, a fine stretch of the wall.

West Street is now a service road for many of the major shops in
Hereford and has a direct access from the Victoria Street section of
the ring road. Formerly it was a dead end, being sealed by one of
the seventeen half-round towers which were a feature of the city
wall. About 1890 the tower was removed to provide access between
West Street and Victoria Street, and Watkins photographed the

resulting sections on each side of the breach. These photographs were an important part of the evidence he was to use some thirty years later in his important paper *The King's Ditch of the City of Hereford*. In this work he postulated several defensive lines around the city which were much earlier than the city wall. Once more he was never to see his theories proved, for it was not until the ring road was built in 1967 that archaeological excavations close to Victoria Street demonstrated the character of the early defences. A few years later further excavations in the garden of a house in Cantilupe Street exposed a well-preserved section of these early defensive works. This section is still open to public view at the rear of St. Owen's Court—the only example of a secular defensive wall of the Saxon period to be displayed anywhere in the country.

Alfred Watkins was meticulous in recording historic buildings when they were being altered or about to be demolished. The resulting photographs are of great help in the understanding of the development of the timber-framed houses of Hereford and for the information they provide about the changes which took place in the city during the late nineteenth and early twentieth centuries. His introduction to a paper on *Three Early Timber Halls in the City of Hereford*, read to Woolhope Club members in 1919, explains why this type of building is still being discovered in the city.

He said 'the subjects of this paper have one common characteristic, besides being of timber construction as was natural in our thickly wooded county. They all became for a considerable period (what remained of them) so incrusted and concealed with modern building and plaster, that any knowledge of their existence practically ceased.'

The three buildings he discussed included the Norman hall of the Bishop's Palace, from which he says that he possessed one of the arches (22ft in external diameter) which was taken out by a builder when Bishop Atlay had alterations made. (Perhaps this is the one which can now be seen underneath the entrance archway leading into the Bishop's Palace.) The hall has been the subject of many papers since this short note by Watkins. He was also impressed by the late fourteenth century Booth Hall, the roof of which had been exposed only a few months earlier; and the hall in Harley Court, where Watkins was then living. He would doubtless have been very happy to know that recent researches have exposed several other buildings of similar antiquity, including the barn at the north-east corner of the Cathedral Close which is of thirteenth century origin; 20 Church Street with its late fourteenth century crown-post roof; and, most recently, an almost complete early fifteenth century roof of a small hall at the rear of 50a Commercial Street.

For most of Watkins' life, the corner of the Ledbury Road with St. Owen Street was considered to be an extremely dangerous bend with hardly any visibility for pedestrians wishing to cross the road. This was due to the seventeenth century St. Giles' Chapel which protruded well out into the junction with Eign Road. This building, recorded both in an article in the Hereford Times and in a series of photographs by Watkins, was demolished in 1927. In excavating the

St. Giles' Chapel at the corner of St. Owen Street and Ledbury Road
from the south-west. The building was demolished in 1927
and rebuilt some distance to the west (Alfred Watkins, 1925)

The site on which St. Giles' Chapel stood with St. Owen Street in the background. The stone foundations visible are those of the twelfth century round Templar church

ground underneath, the foundations of a round church were discovered. A further series of photographs were taken and it was hoped that the remains could be preserved. In the event this was not possible, but Watkins managed to persuade the then city surveyor to design the new boundary wall of the gardens, where it adjoins the road, to sit on an arc of the old foundation some thirteen feet in length. This stretch of wall still survives with its small plaque reading 'The stones below are part of the walls of the twelfth century round chapel of Saint Giles, found in 1927 when demolishing the chapel of 1682'.

Another part of this twelfth century building to survive is the carved tympanum, showing Christ in Majesty, incongruously placed in the side wall of the adjoining almshouses. The detailed photograph taken by Watkins provides a good indication of the extent of weathering, during the last sixty years, of this important example of the Herefordshire School of Carving.

The Romanesque tympanum from the nearby round church, now built into a side wall of St. Giles' Almshouses in St. Owen Street, (Alfred Watkins)

One building with which Watkins was intimately connected still survives and is probably the most photographed building in the city after the cathedral. This is the Old House in High Town, now a museum providing visitors with an insight into seventeenth century life in Hereford.

High Town, originally a large triangular market place created by William FitzOsbern, Earl of Hereford, directly after the Norman Conquest, contained two churches, St. Peter's to the east and All Saints to the west. When it was built it was one of the largest market places in the country, giving some indication of the importance attached to Hereford in the latter part of the eleventh century.

Gradually the market stalls which filled it became more permanent structures and later rows of timber-framed shops with dwellings above occupied most of the area. In parts they remain (such as between Eign Gate and Bewell Street) but those in High Town were gradually demolished at the beginning of the nineteenth century leaving the Old House (built in 1621) as an isolated reminder of what had been known as Cooken Row and Butchers Row.

Cooken Row faced onto the north side of High Town and was where the bakers and confectioners plied their trade. Most of these buildings were demolished by 1818. Butchers Row stood back-to-back with Cooken Row and was separated from the Old House by a narrow, rather dark passage known incongruously as Golden Alley. It was here that animals were slaughtered in the street and meat sold. Adjoining the Old House on the east was the Old George Inn which spent its declining years as a butcher's shop. All the buildings, with the exception of the Old House, were demolished by 1837.

Alfred Watkins would have seen the Old House with a variety of different occupants. For many years it had been used as a saddlers shop, but in 1872 Matthew Oatfield's hardware business moved in and occupied this prime site for ten years. In 1882 the building was bought by the Worcester City and County Banking Company, later absorbed by Lloyd's Bank. By 1928 Lloyd's had built a new banking chamber on the north side of High Town and most generously made a gift of the Old House to the city on condition that it was not used for commercial purposes.

The city council decided that the building should be used as a museum but much work was needed, first to remove the floors and fittings of Lloyd's Bank and then to reinstate the interior of the house as it had been originally. The work was organised by the Old House Committee of the city council, Watkins being one of the leading members. It was he who wrote the first guide to the building, which was eventually published in June 1934. It contained ten illustrations, all taken from his own photographs. Another member of the committee, Mr. M.C. Oatfield, who had lived in the house as a child, contributed one hundred guineas towards the restoration costs, and the guide book acknowledges this gift and the keen interest and generosity of people both in the county and in the city of Hereford, not confined to one class, but ranging from cottager to mansion dweller, each ready to lend or give his piece of old furnishing.

In the 1930's the Old House was open on a daily basis with an admission charge of 6 pence for adults and 3 pence for children. Each Thursday admission was free, by request of the Director of the

The Old House in High Town when it was still the hardware shop of Matthew Oatfield

Victoria and Albert Museum (who provided grants and furniture). Free admission has continued one day each week to the present time although the entrance charges have increased somewhat.

The 1934 guide book was revised several times and has now been totally replaced by a modern guide. One section, which was printed in the first edition, was dropped in later ones. It is worth including here for it gives a good impression of this part of Hereford in the latter part of the nineteenth century, and of Watkins' feelings.

There was, he wrote 'The sight of the "Old House Pigeons" who in the time of John Roberts—the saddler—made their home in the roof, and many a savoury pie of the young squabs the old man enjoyed in consequence. They fed in the streets, in days when leavings from horse-traffic was more acceptable to bird picking than those from motor engines. The pigeons were turned out of the house in 1872, but found shelter in the belfry of St. Peter's Church.

Again they were evicted but a remnant still come to the yards of the two flour-mills in the city for pickings.

'Once a year the birds gather for a memorable occasion. The appointed hour of the morning of Armistice Day is near, the people are drifting towards the war memorial cross in St. Peter's Square. The sound of prayer and hymn is heard: it is an unusual item in bird-life: and these town pigeons are assembled in ranks of expectation on the tower parapet. There is a hush around the cross, broken by the deep signal boom of the maroon, when the birds rise with startled unison in one swoop of curved formation and loud clapping of wings. In the two minutes' silence they quietly come back for the second signal, and with the dispersing crowd they too depart, not again to gather at this vantage-point until, in a year's time, there comes once more the eleventh day of the eleventh month.

'There come back, too, memories of past times when horse-cabs stood in the ranks where motor cars now wait for hire, and where the old Butchers Row and Market Place once stood. Very striking then the effect when, on a wet night, the lights of shop windows and cab rank were reflected in the rain-drenched square.

'The yearly orgy of May Fair gave a new aspect to this Old House, for all round were booths, stalls and roundabouts, whilst Fossett's Photographic Studio long took up its position almost blocking the bank entrance.'

High Town is no longer the main thoroughfare for east-west traffic passing through Hereford and the whole area has become a pedestrian precinct. The cabs have been banished from outside the Old House, but the pigeons still remain.

VI

The County Record Photographer

The young Alfred Watkins would have been able to wander around the streets of Hereford with much more freedom than the modern day youngster. Although many of the roads in the central part of the city had been widened with the demolition of Butchers Row, Cooken Row and the Market Hall all in High Town, the old St. Nicholas' Church at the corner of King Street and Bridge Street and, of course, the city gates, traffic still moved slowly and did not present a great hazard to a young child. Travel outside the city would have been much more restricted—although the railway had arrived, the local destinations were limited and this was a period well before the mass annual exodus to the seaside.

Watkins began to roam around the county when he started work as an outrider (the local word for a traveller) for his father's brewery. His mode of transport during the 1870's was a horse and gig. This was one of the most pleasant and leisurely ways of travelling around the countryside, being sufficiently slow to see and appreciate everything in the surrounding fields. The horse would doubtless have needed little encouragement to stop whilst, from his later writings, it's clear that Watkins needed even less inducement.

In one of his later articles in the Hereford Times in 1927 he mentions the old coach road from Hereford to Leominster at Dinmore Hill. He observes that 'On this road, if you look on the face of a rock, on the left before you get to the dangerous bend— (year after year a blue tit built her nest here when I was a lad)—you will see that old travellers have recorded their passing. "No more

Watkins' name, which he carved on a rock on Dinmore Hill at the rate of one letter a month during 1876

this way" is one, and we wonder why L.M., who cut his record on Jan. 2nd, 1829, ceased passing, for another traveller I knew, who drove over the hill once a month calling at the inns for his father's brewery, also cut his full name half a century ago (in 1876), but could only do one letter a month, his nag being restive, so it took a year to finish. And this traveller is still occasionally "on the road" doing trade journeys.'

He would regularly pass the time of day with people he met, irrespective of their status. He must also have taken every opportunity to examine churches, castles and other historic buildings when he visited the more remote parts of Herefordshire. It was not to be long before he started carrying his camera with him.

After a few years at this work he changed from travelling for the brewery business to working for his father's flour mill. This continued to provide him with the opportunities to travel around the county, now visiting many isolated farms and villages and gleaning much useful information.

His first sortie into the field of publication came in 1882 when he supplied the illustrations for a guide book called *Hereford, Herefordshire and The Wye*, written by D.R. Chapman. Mr. Chapman was the librarian and curator of the Hereford Free Library and Museum in Broad Street. The book, of which five hundred copies were printed for general sale, was dedicated to James Rankin Esq., who was not only member of parliament for Leominster and chief steward of the city, but was also the founder of the library. There were eight illustrations in the book, all taken from photographs by Alfred Watkins. He also assisted the author in the compilation of the many walks in the county which are described in the book.

The book is, in many ways, typical of its period and was designed to cater for the increasing number of people with sufficient leisure time to travel around the countryside and visit the acknowledged beauty spots. However, three copies were very special productions. Each of them contained thirty-three additional illustrations in permanent platinotype, photographed by Watkins. Hereford is fortunate in possessing one of these copies which was presented to the city library by the author and photographer on publication. The additional photographs cover a wide variety of subjects and provide a unique picture of life in Herefordshire in the latter part of the nineteenth century. Many villages and buildings are included, such as the market place at Pembridge, street scenes in Ledbury, Eardisland and Weobley, the toll gate at Whitney and the old grammar school at Kington. All Saints Church in Hereford, the old church at Downton and Llanthony Priory show Watkins' interest in religious buildings. However, the photographs which stand out most are the ones depicting countryside events—a Herefordshire hop-garden, the hay-mill at Downton, and two simply labelled as 'a farm-yard scene' and 'a cottage scene'.

The first major piece of research compiled by Watkins alone and marking his debut as an author, was published in *The English Illustrated Magazine*. It was entitled *A Summer amongst the Dovecots* and included a series of line drawings by C.M. Gere and E.H. New of the most important examples, taken from his own photographs. In the article he explains that 'It was with the idea of forming a record of these curious buildings, that I resolved to collect particulars of all in my own county. Many a pleasant tramp, camera on back, through orchard and fallow, along by-roads, over wooded hills, and past thatched cottages, this search entailed.' The article was extended and printed as a booklet in 1891 by William Pollard and Co. of Exeter. This is now very rare as only seventy-five copies were published—all for private circulation. The article was accompanied with an appendix containing a list of all the pigeon houses in Herefordshire visited by the author during 1888 and 1889. This list of some seventy-four dovecots includes the type, detailed measurements, the number of nest holes, and, wherever possible, details of dating. He also provided a list of lost pigeon houses, with approximate dates of their demolition.

Following a talk on the subject to the members of the Woolhope Club, this article was reprinted for a second time in the *Transactions* of the society for 1890-2. Watkins presented the frontispiece for this volume which includes two of his earliest photographs—the pigeon house at Wigmore Grange taken in 1878 before its demolition in 1888, and that at Putson which was demolished in 1878.

Watkins wrote his article to provide a permanent record of this class of buildings and in doing so he anticipated, by some ninety years, a recent publication by the county council on the same subject. The reasons he gave for his survey are just as valid today, when many redundant barns, small country churches and chapels are being abandoned often with minimal recording, as dovecots were in the latter part of the nineteenth century. He said of the dovecots 'In our county there are still a large number of interesting examples left, but each decade lessens the number, and out of a list of thirty-four demolished pigeon houses which I have compiled, not one has, to my knowledge, been described or illustrated. Of the seventy-four existing examples which I have surveyed (and photographed for the most part) only one, that at Garway, had previously been described. It was this consideration which induced me to make as complete a survey as possible.'

For many years after this publication, Watkins only went into print about subjects close to his heart and within his home county.

Pigeon House and
Falconry at
Buttas

PIGEON HOUSE, THE MOOR FARM, HEREFORD.

*Drawings of pigeon houses used in Watkins' first major published work.
The drawings were taken from his original photographs as photographic
reproduction was still uncommon in the early 1890's*

The sixteen feet square timber-framed pigeon house at Putson near Hereford which was demolished in 1889 (Alfred Watkins, 1888)

These articles, which were published from time to time in the *Transactions* of the Woolhope Club, cover a wide range of topics. He also continued to take many photographs on his frequent visits to the various parts of the county, whether out on business or when taking part in the field trips of the Woolhope Club.

One of the earlier articles was entitled *The Strange Story of Wisteston Chapel.* Wisteston adjoins the parish of Marden, some six miles north of Hereford. Apparently the chapel was built in 1715 by a John Price on his own freehold land but within the Wisteston Court estate. He claimed that it was built on the site of an old chapel long since demolished and therefore did not require to be consecrated. His story must have been believed for the governors of Queen Anne's Bounty agreed to augment the chapel, the first grant being £200 in 1726. (This bounty was created to replace the income lost when glebe land, which had originally provided the vicar with tithes, was disposed of.)

The chapel was restored in 1860, and after 1870 was used from time to time by the Watkins family who had by then moved to Wisteston Court. It was only used for occasional services and by 1885 it was once again in bad repair and disused. Little repair work appears to have been done, although in 1888 Watkins' father left £25 in his will towards a fund for that purpose. Eventually, in 1894, an attempt was made by the owner to sell the building. He said that the chapel was no longer wanted and would no doubt fall into ruin. The payments from Queen Anne's Bounty were suspended shortly afterwards as no services were being performed. Apparently the dean and chapter then purchased the advowson and in 1909 Canon Capes was appointed to the living, which was treated as a perpetual curacy. The following year the chapel was totally demolished. There were several burials in a vault within the chapel and these were

Wisteston Chapel from the north-west shortly before it was demolished
(Alfred Watkins, 1910)

taken to Sutton St. Michael for re-burial in one grave. Wisteston thus joined the long list of Herefordshire churches which have disappeared over the ages but, due to the efforts of Alfred Watkins, it is not entirely forgotten.

In two successive years, 1916 and 1917, Watkins read two important and related papers to members of the Woolhope Club. The first dealt with *Herefordshire Churchyard Crosses*, whilst the second considered the position and nature of *Herefordshire Wayside and Town Crosses*. Each article was profusely illustrated by his own photographs—a record which is now of immense historical and archaeological value, for many of these crosses have disappeared or been damaged in the last seventy years. The survey must have taken much time and effort, for there was no previous complete record and Watkins must have had to visit every town and village in the county and talk to the older villagers to establish the position and history of each individual cross.

Watkins' interests in crosses may have stemmed from his childhood when he walked the two miles or so out of Hereford on the Hay road to see the remains of the White Cross. This may well have been used as a market cross during the fourteenth century after the second visitation of the Black Death, and tradition has it that it was erected for this purpose by Bishop Charleton. Watkins recalls making a clay model of it before it was restored in 1867, and makes very unfavourable comments about the 'flag-staff-like shaft added out of all proportion' which meant that 'the cross of my childhood seemed spoilt for ever to me'. The restoration work was supervised by the eminent, if rather heavy-handed architect, Sir Gilbert Scott. The several photographs taken of this cross by Watkins will be of great help during the next restoration, which will have to take place in the near future or all the carving's details will be completely lost.

But Watkins was not just interested in recording the details of each cross, he was also concerned about their long term future. Thus, at both Tyberton and Madley, where the churchyard crosses are of considerable interest, a committee of three, composed of Rev. G.W. Turner, Canon Bannister and Watkins himself, was formed to restore the cross-heads.

The White Cross after it had 'the flag-staff-like shaft' added
(Alfred Watkins)

95

Most cross-heads had been damaged or completely destroyed during the Reformation and only a few examples survive in situ to the present day. The history of the Madley head, as given by Watkins, illustrates the problems of survival and gives an insight into the investigatory research which went in to the production of his article. The cross-head had apparently lain buried in the church-yard for many years, possibly having been lost at the Reformation. Then 'Many years ago some men working for the late Mr. Edward Bigglestone, a Hereford monumental mason, brought it back from Madley when fixing a headstone there. A Mrs. Lane who lived in Portland Street, begged it from Mr. Bigglestone to ornament her

The churchyard cross at Bosbury with its mid-seventeenth century inscription
(Alfred Watkins, 1917)

The cross-head at Sellack, north of Ross (Alfred Watkins, 1929)

garden. Her brother-in-law, Mr. Tom Maddy, saw it there, and in his turn begged it from Mrs. Lane. Mr. Maddy, who was foreman for our late Assistant Secretary (of the Woolhope Club), Mr. Robert Clarke, gave it to his employer. After Mr. Clarke's death, his widow gave it in charge to the committee to replace it in its right position.'

The only two churchyard crosses to be left in place following the wholesale destruction of the 1640's were those at Bosbury and Sellack. In the first case, the condition for retention was that the words: HONOUR NOT THE † BUT HONOUR GOD FOR CHRIST should be engraved on it. The cross, with the words still legible, survives to the present day. At Sellack, one of the most delightful and unspoilt of our Herefordshire villages, the local vicar, the Reverend Pritchard tried an even more successful ploy. He entertained the troop of soldiers, sent to destroy the cross and the recently installed stained glass window, so well that they desisted from their sacrilegious intent.

In relatively recent years the cross-heads at Hentland, Putley, King's Capel and Knill have been found and replaced on their broken shafts and at Tedstone Delamere the head is built in to the churchyard wall. A fragment of the head at Yarkhill is built into the church wall in a dark place in the porch, whilst the fragment of an elegant cross preserved in Upton Bishop church, which has been used as a pattern for several new cross heads within the county, is probably the finial from a gable.

Many years later, Watkins was to accumulate the results of the many hours of labour which had produced his two papers in a book *The Old Standing Crosses of Herefordshire*, published by Simkin Marshall Ltd. for the Woolhope Club in 1930. In the preface he comments, rather wryly, that he had opened more churchyard gates than books during his researches. Every cross and cross-base is illustrated, many by the photographs from his earlier visits, but others taken during his later visits in 1928 and 1929 when he was in his 70's. The schedule of existing crosses is impressive—a total of one hundred and twenty—all recorded in considerable detail with exact measurements of all the surviving parts.

Most of Watkins' photographs were taken many years before the first reasonably complete survey of the county was undertaken by the Royal Commission on Ancient and Historical Monuments in the late 1920's and early 1930's, so providing information and evidence that otherwise would have been lost. Earlier attempts had been made by Duncumb who started his *Collections towards a History of Herefordshire* in 1804. This was far from complete on his death and in any event was too early to include photographic illustrations. The much later *Victoria County History of Herefordshire* published in 1906 was planned as a series, but never progressed beyond the first volume.

All these sources provide the basic framework for all serious researchers into the history and archaeology of Herefordshire, but what can often be lost to posterity are details of the casual finds such as the fleeting glimpses of historic buildings exposed during restorations, coins found during building works, and buried remains unearthed during excavations for new buildings and roads. Watkins, constantly advised by his large collection of friends and acquaintances, made every effort to record and photograph such events and then publish the results in the annual Archaeological Reports of the Woolhope *Transactions*. He edited this section from its inception in 1917 until his death, a period of eighteen years. These reports are full of interest and are all well illustrated; they contain the snippets of information which may not have been of any great significance at the time, but which may, many years later, give the clue to some otherwise insignificant event or pattern.

Just a few examples of Watkins' records give some impression of the variety of his observations. In 1917 he notes that Holme Lacy

The interior of the church at Clodock looking east with its seventeenth century box pews before restoration (Alfred Watkins, 1917)

Church had its walls underpinned and the floor levels lowered—this could well save future archaeologists much time and effort, for they will know that most archaeological levels will have been either badly disturbed or totally removed. The same issue contains an internal photograph of Clodock Church before the 'ill-kept, dirty, decayed interior of this large mother church' was restored. During the restoration the large box pews were re-ordered to make for easier access.

In 1921 he recorded Roman finds from the Blackwardine area, a cross-slab found during rebuilding works at the Castle Inn, Ewyas Harold, and Roman remains from Leintwardine. The following year he went out to Peterchurch to record and photograph the fourteenth century roof and other features exposed during restoration work at Wellbrook Farm. Typically he walked around the area and noted a rectilinear earthwork and a mound or tumulus in the orchard at the rear of the house. Two years later he had to record the destruction of the tumulus.

In 1924 he recorded old trackways at Eardisland, Shelwick and Sutton Walls all of which he related to his new ley-line theories. The probability of a Roman site at Westhide is mentioned in both 1926 and in 1927, and in the latter year a fragment of Saxon cross found near Blakemere is illustrated.

In 1931 Watkins included in his report a note concerning his researches into early pottery production sites in Herefordshire. This was in effect an appendix to a series of articles he had written and illustrated on the subject which went back as far as 1917. Knowledge of early pottery kilns is of great significance to modern archaeologists interested in the methods of production and the distances that the wares would have travelled from their sources to the final points of use. From this type of information a picture of late medieval and earlier trading patterns is now beginning to emerge. The first essential is to have available the earlier records of the sources of the individual wares, and Watkins' records provide this information for Herefordshire and is constantly referred to at the present day.

The various potteries noted by him include one discovered in 1916 by the son of the station master at Whitney in the aptly named Kiln Ground Wood which was 'being cut down by Finns employed by the government and encamped here'. Many examples are described of this well-made and well-distributed seventeenth century pottery.

It took several visits to Grove Head at Lingen before Watkins and several of his friends found the spoil heaps which were associated with this pottery production site on the banks of the Limebrook within the ancient Deerfold Forest. Samples of this early seventeenth century ware were collected and are illustrated in photographs. Another of these seventeenth century 'cottage industries' was discovered near Kempley in 1928. Two more sites followed in 1931 as interest grew. These were at Strangworth Farm at Titley, and at Birtley near Lingen.

Researches of this nature tend to lead to an increase in interest and encourage people to report any new discoveries. Fragments of pottery brought to Watkins by a Mr. Betteridge in 1931 led to the finding of the first Herefordshire example of a Romano-British kiln-site near Marley Hall, north-west of Ledbury. Interest continued to grow, for in the same year the traces of two clay pipe production

Pottery fragments recovered from Birtley, Lingen (Alfred Watkins, 1931)

101

centres were found on remote sites in the county. One, at the appropriately named Pipe Aston, was known by repute although the precise site was not discovered till a wagon wheel had to be dug out of soft ground; the second was at Birtley Farm at Lingen. Clay pipes, with their distinctive manufacturer's stamps, have since been studied in great detail and provide a useful dating tool for archaeologists working in the post-medieval period.

Even in his late 70's Watkins was still out and about in the country areas taking photographs of longstones, cup-marked stones and stone mortars. The 1933 Woolhope Club archaeology report includes no less than twenty-three of his photographs taken in many parts of the county.

His most famous book *The Old Straight Track* is not only a book about ley lines. It also contains well over a hundred photographic illustrations, mostly taken in Herefordshire and the surrounding areas. The book was first published in 1925 and is still in print—it was the culmination of over half a century's familiarity with a region he loved so well.

Drinking tea next to the hawker's van (Alfred Watkins)

The hawker's van which travelled around Herefordshire selling baskets (Alfred Watkins)

Osier-stripping, a long-lost Herefordshire industry (Alfred Watkins)

Children hop-picking (Alfred Watkins, 1903)

Hop-picking at Dilwyn. The man on the left has a string of tally sticks around his neck (Alfred Watkins, 1903)

A mobile cider-press (Alfred Watkins)

Ledbury: The High Street from the south (Alfred Watkins)

Ledbury: High Street from below the Market Hall (Alfred Watkins)

VII

The Woolhope Club

The Woolhope Naturalists' Field Club was formed in 1851 for the practical study of the natural history, in all its branches, of Herefordshire and the districts immediately adjacent. It takes its name from the Woolhope Dome, an area to the east of Hereford which is of great interest to geologists. The fine ideals of the original members have continued through to the present day for the Woolhope Club is still thriving with its members continuing their researches in the fields of archaeology, botany, ornithology and other such subjects.

Alfred Watkins was proposed and elected a member of the club on 24 May 1888, Queen Victoria's 69th Birthday. The club was having an outdoor meeting in the Kington area on that day and the formal business, which included his election, was carried out on the summit of Stanner Hill.

The *Transactions* of the club provide many details of the regular meetings held during the latter part of the nineteenth and the early twentieth centuries and of the research which the members carried out during their field outings. From these we learn the first meeting that Watkins attended was an annual meeting held in the Club Room in the library and museum building in Broad Street—where the club still meets. This building was provided by the generosity of Sir James Rankin, a member of the club, on the understanding that the Woolhopians should have a permanent home in the building.

Once each year the club held a Ladies Day when the wives and daughters of members were invited to participate in a field trip.

Watkins first took his wife to one such meeting during June 1889 when the club went to Newland in the Forest of Dean. The secretary recorded this outing as 'one of the happiest days which the annals of the Woolhope Club have been able to place upon record.' The fifty or so members were accommodated in a special carriage to Newland, and the officials of the Great Western Railway Company ran a special return train from Monmouth at 6.15 p.m. to enable members to catch evening trains home from Hereford. On the outward journey there was a stop at Ross to visit the garden of the president of the club at The Graig; and a second stop at Monmouth for a tour around the town. Then on by train again to Newland, where carriages were in readiness to take the party to the Great Oak Tree near Newland House. The tree was measured, being forty-three feet six inches around at five feet above the ground—a real monster of an oak!

Whilst they were there several papers on oak trees and associated folklore were read to the assemblage. It was suggested that the age of an oak may be determined from the old ryhme:

> Three hundred years the oak expends in growth,
> Three hundred years in majesty stands forth,
> Three hundred years declines and wastes away
> Then dies, and takes three hundred to decay.

However it was not surprisingly agreed that a scientific count of tree rings would be more accurate.

Folklore, then as now, was of great interest. The relative merits of:

> If the Oak is in leaf before the Ash,
> 'Twill be dry, and warm, and good wheat to thrash;
> If the Ash is in leaf before the Oak,
> 'Twill be cold, and of rain too great a soak;
> If the Oak and the Ash open their leaves together,
> Expect a summer of changeable weather.

And the almost opposite:

The Newland oak tree visited by Woolhope Club members in 1889
(Alfred Watkins)

> If the Oak is out before the Ash,
> 'Twill be a summer of wet and splash;
> But if the Ash is before the Oak,
> 'Twill be a summer of fire and smoke.

Many observations on the timing of spring across the whole of the country were read and discussed whilst the members stood around the Newland Oak. The final comment, perhaps inevitably, had also to be in a rhyme of sorts:

> The Ash being out before the Oak
> Is nothing better than a joke.

The carriages then went on to St. Briavel's. The weather was good and the roads were dusty—the *Transactions* wryly record 'It was remarkable that more than one lady's hair had turned grey in three-quarters of an hour.' The church and the castle were visited, and are described in some detail in the *Transactions*, before the party continued on their journey back towards Monmouth, diverting slightly by Sling's Pit to visit 'one of the "scowles" or "workings of the old men" as the Foresters term them, being traces of Roman workings in their search for iron ore.'

Watkins went on one more visit the same year, when the club had a joint meeting with the Malvern Field Club in the Malvern Hills area. There they examined several geological formations, finding several fossils, and then continued to the top of the hills for a walk around the ramparts of the Iron Age hillforts at British Camp and Midsummer Hill.

The annual meeting in April 1890 was the occasion when Watkins read his first paper to the members gathered in the club room. This was entitled *Herefordshire Pigeon-houses* and the Woolhopians had a rare treat, for Watkins, 'by means of the oxy-hydrogen lantern, reproduced upon the screen a series of photographs, the results of many years' observations.' To produce this effect heavy cylinders of oxygen and hydrogen would have had to be carried up the stairs to the first-floor clubroom, and the complicated business of persuading the lantern to work efficiently would have taken considerable time. Had this not been enough he could well have been nervous during his presentation for one member of the audience was the Reverend Bowell who had been his headmaster at the Widemarsh Gatehouse School!

It was some time before he went on another expedition with the club, possibly in part due to the births of his two children. But in October 1891 he attended one of their famous 'Fungus Forays'. These were regular yearly events and the early issues of the *Transactions* are well illustrated with colour and black-and-white illustrations of the enthusiasts' findings. The meeting Watkins attended was in Paradise Wood at Pontrilas.

In August 1892 he spent a day with club members on a visit to the Brecon Beacons. The railway from Hereford to Brecon, which had been opened in 1860, was then still thriving. (It was to close almost a hundred years after its inception.) The directions for organising this type of event and the views to be seen from the train give some indication of the changes in administration of our railways, and the loss we have suffered from the closure of this line and the one which crossed the Beacons themselves.

The secretary, in his report in the *Transactions*, tells us 'Having guaranteed a party of say fifty members, you must request the Midland Railway Company to make arrangements with the Brecon and Merthyr Railway Company to give you a special train along their line from Talyllyn Junction to Torpantau. Proceeding along this latter line, the first station from Talyllyn is Talybont, a pretty village near the junction of the River Cafanog with the Usk. Upon the left are seen: Llangorse Lake, the largest lake, except Bala, in the whole of Wales, being three miles in length, one and a half miles broad; the Mynydd Troed range of hills; and, in the left background, the range of the Black Mountains, terminating in the conical peak of Crow's Foot, stretching far away in the distant horizon.

'... Reaching the summit of the ascent, the train enters a tunnel, immediately on emergence from which the traveller finds himself landed on the platform of the railway station at Torpantau, at an elevation of 1,314 feet above the sea. There is no refreshment room at the station, nor are any to be found on the Beacons, you will therefore act wisely in soliciting the assistance of the gude-wife of the station master to prepare a good fire, hot water, and other creature comforts, in event of your return to Torpantau.'

Botany, ornithology and geology were all studied during the day and all the peaks visible from the summit of Pen-y-Fan are listed. Half of the party returned to Torpantau (and sat down to afternoon tea prepared by the station master's wife) whilst the more active members walked to Brecon.

Watkins again took his wife to a Ladies Day meeting in 1893. For this outing the train was taken to New Radnor and a wagonette was provided by the Eagle Inn, for those who needed it, for the two-and-a-half mile journey to the charmingly named Water-break-its-neck. Ladies days were popular and the following year he and his wife went again, this time to Church Stretton for a seven mile walk to the Longmynd. It was during 1894 that Watkins was elected to the central committee of the Woolhope Club.

A different type of meeting was held in June 1896 when ninety members and friends made a first visit to the works of the proprietors of the Birmingham Water Supply at Elan Valley. This was certainly a meeting that Watkins would not have wanted to miss for this was the beginning of a very large scale project which would eventually involve the drowning of several of the mid-Wales valleys. The train was taken to Rhayader where Mr. Hope Edwards, of the Royal Inn, provided eighty-five seats in his carriages for the remainder of the journey 'in a manner creditable to this little town.'

The railway companies continued to be helpful in 1897 when the venue was the Wyre Forest. A special carriage for members of the club was put on the train from Hereford to avoid them having to change at Wooferton Junction on their way to Wyre Forest station.

Watkins decided to take a hand in policy decisions of the club in 1897 when he proposed that each year the *Transactions* should be printed and issued to members at, or immediately after, the end of the year rather than every two or three years as was the practice.

The middle dam in the Elan Valley waterworks scheme during construction
(Alfred Watkins, 1899)

Building the submerged dam at the Elan Valley waterworks
(Alfred Watkins, 1899)

This motion was not successful—'the Central Committee decided with regret that they could not see their way to adopt Mr. Watkins' proposition.'

The volume of the *Transactions* for the period 1898-99 was the first to contain many photographs. Presumably the printers, Jakeman and Carver of 4 & 5 High Town, Hereford, had obtained new machinery allowing the economic production of photographic plates. Watkins provided ten photographs for this volume, including a magnificent series showing the work in progress on the Elan dams in 1899. The club had invited members and officials of the Hereford Corporation on this, their second visit to the project. Early starts were the order of the day for Woolhopians—they caught the 7.25 a.m. train from Hereford to reach Rhayader at 9.20. From Rhayader the group, numbering over a hundred people, was accommodated in six open trucks with plank seats. They travelled on the ten miles of the Birmingham Corporation railway, built since their previous visit, and were allowed half-an-hour at each of the four

Elan Valley—the submerged dam and bridge when complete
(Alfred Watkins)

dams so as not to clash with the regular trains. The whole project had started in 1893 and completion was anticipated in 1902, so the work was more than half finished when this second visit was made.

The club's motto 'Hope on, hope ever' was, perhaps, strained a little towards the end of this particular day. Many of the members decided not to wait until 3.30 p.m. for their president and distinguished guests to arrive for the repast, prepared on several tables under a canvas tent at the Elan Valley Hotel. Their excuse was that they had to catch the 3.50 train from Rhayader—the report of the meeting records the difficulty of raising a quorum to give the health of the Queen and to thank the resident engineers for all their help!

Watkins was elected a vice-president of the club for the year 1899, in recognition of his photographic work and of his increasing involvement in the management and organisation of the society.

The Woolhope Club did not always meet in distant parts of the county or beyond, and in 1900 there were two local meetings, both attended by Watkins. The first, in June, was to Stoke Edith, Perton

The northern side of the chancel at Craswall Priory showing the piscina and sedilla. The site had just been excavated when this photograph was taken (Alfred Watkins, 1904)

and Dormington. Even then the train was used—to Stoke Edith station on the outward journey and from Withington station for the return to Hereford. The day included an eight mile walk, as far as the Iron Age camp on Backbury Hill, and dinner, by courtesy of Mr. and Mrs. Scott Hall, under an awning on the lawn of Dormington Court. Watkins must have carried his heavy photographic gear with him for he photographed Dormington quarry and the fine medieval door-knocker at Dormington Church.

The second meeting was an extra one held in Hereford to visit the cathedral, chained library and Mappa Mundi and to examine the vestiges of the city walls. Was this when Watkins began to be interested in the evolution of the defences of Hereford, which was eventually to result in several papers for the *Transactions?*

A meeting in 1904 at Lyonshall gave him the chance to read another paper, this time on the subject of Offa's Dyke. The party had taken the train from Hereford to Lyonshall and, after viewing the castle and church, went on to examine the traces of the famous dyke built by Offa in the eighth century. From there they went to Almeley for tea and refreshments at the vicarage, and then to Eardisley for dinner at the New Inn. After dinner Watkins read his paper *Offa's Dyke: The Gap in the Weobley District.* He admitted to spending many half-days walking in the area looking for traces of the dyke between Yazor and Lyonshall. The paper led to a long discussion after which the party, some fifty strong, caught the early evening train from Eardisley station back to Hereford.

Later in 1904 the club visited one of the most inaccessible parts of Herefordshire, where they saw the excavations conducted by C.J. Lilwall at the ruins of the Grandmontine priory at Craswall. This is one of the most remote of the many monastic sites in the country and one of only three houses of the Grandmontine Order in England. To reach Craswall the party, some sixty strong, walked up from Hay starting about ten o'clock in the morning. On their arrival at the priory, Lilwall read a paper on his work, photographs were taken, and the visitors continued to Craswall Church. The walk had covered some eight miles and, although it was then 2.30, the stalwart members 'could not resist the temptation' to ascend Hay Bluff before returning to Hay for a 4.30 luncheon at the Crown Hotel.

Watkins must have found Lilwall's work of great interest for he took several photographs at the time and accompanied club members on a second visit to examine the extended excavations and take further photographs in 1908. Because of the remoteness of the site, there had been little stone-robbing since the priory was abandoned in 1442. All that had happened was that the roofs of the main buildings had collapsed and the walls, which survived in places to wall-plate level, were thus buried under the piles of debris. It is unfortunate that the substantial remains cleared by Lilwall were left open to the elements without any attempt at conservation. In the eighty or so years since Lilwall completed his work the exposed masonry has suffered considerably. Watkins' photographs will be of great help in providing the essential details for the consolidation works which are now being planned for this important site.

The remains of the doorway leading from the cloisters into the chapter house at Craswall Priory after excavation by Lilwall (Alfred Watkins, 1908)

At the beginning of July 1908 the club visited the Capel-y-ffin and Llanthony area, where Watkins read a short paper on a dovecot within the domestic buildings of the priory that he had discovered during an earlier visit. This was the first time that he was accompanied by his son Allen, then some 19 years old, and though Allen was to accompany his father on several other club expeditions, he never became a member in his own right.

The *Transactions* for the years 1912-13 include an appendix on the excavations by G.H. Jack at the Roman town of Kenchester, some five miles west of Hereford. The preface notes that 'One feature of the present volume is the vivid excellence of the photographic illustrations, in which details of sculpture etc. can be traced as distinctly as if one stood personally before the objects represented.' With only one exception, all the photographs in both the volume and the appendix were taken by Watkins.

There was only one volume of the *Transactions* issued during the four years of the First World War, but it is of some interest as it includes several papers written by Watkins. During these war years he was again elected as vice-president and also became a member of the editorial committee of the club.

In 1917, the club decided that the *Transactions* should include annual reports from the sectional editors, and Watkins contributed the section on archaeology from that date until his death.

The suggestion which he had made many years previously that the *Transactions* should be published annually, was finally accepted in 1918, and three annual parts now go to make each complete volume. During the same year the central committee considered the question of ladies becoming members of the club. They decided 'that the indiscriminate admission of ladies would seriously interfere with the scientific objects for which the club was founded'! Apparently this was not entirely to Watkins' satisfaction for when elected president for the year 1919 he seconded a motion (which was not accepted) that two ladies should be elected as members.

As president he must have felt that he should increase his contributions to the *Transactions*, and in 1919 and 1920 he provided no less than six papers on such diverse subjects as the defences of Hereford, the brooks called Eign, and Garway Church.

In the early 1920's Watkins, by then in his late 60's, continued to provide the majority of the photographs used in the *Transactions* and attended most of the club meetings. The *Transactions* for 1922 has as a frontispiece a coloured plate of the early fourteenth century stained glass window at Eaton Bishop Church which had been made from an autochrome photograph taken by him.

For the next two years his main contributions to the *Transactions* were his photographs and the archaeology recorder's reports. The latter were full of interest—prehistoric finds, Roman remains, historic buildings—all indicating his continual observation of the post-war regeneration of the county and his contacts with a vast circle of friends. The gap in published papers during this period may well have been due to his preoccupation with ley lines. Many of his later lectures and papers are concerned with this topic, but although he had taken up a new interest, he subsequently found time for several other papers such as the reports on the discovery of several pottery production sites and his talk on *Elizabeth Barrett and Hope End*. He had wanted to extend the latter into a book entitled *Masefield Country* but this was never completed.

The well-planned visits by train gradually came to an end with the advent of the motor car and the char-a-banc which was increasingly used after the war. Thus, on the Ladies Day visit to Eardisley, Clifford and Bredwardine in 1928, they drove much of the way, only walking from Middlewood over Merbach (for the magnificent views) and then via Arthur's Stone down to Bredwardine. The following meeting, in southern Herefordshire, included a visit to Caradoc Court, where the visitors were entertained to tea. Watkins took several photographs of the fifteenth century timber-framed parts of the building which are now being used as an aid to reconstruction work following the disastrous fire in 1986.

The vexed question of the admission of ladies to the club was again discussed at a special general meeting in 1931. Watkins spoke at length in favour of their admission and was reported as saying that 'He remembered the time when almost everyone who joined

Caradoc Court at Sellack, since gutted by fire. This photograph shows the timber framework on the riverside elevation (Alfred Watkins, 1928)

the club used a microscope and was seriously interested in photography. To-day the craft of photography was dead ... the study of botany and of mycology was also almost dead. There had, however, been a tremendous change in another direction—women were waking up and taking an interest in the things which men had dropped.'

His suggestion that the club was a dying society was received with loud cries of dissent and, despite his impassioned plea, the motion to admit ladies was lost by 46 votes to 11. Ladies were not to be admitted as full members until after his death.

He read a most useful paper to club members in December 1931 which was based on his memories of Hereford going back over seventy years. *Hereford Place-names and Sites* provides modern day archaeologists and historians with an important reference list of streets, ancient sites, official buildings, cross-sites, gates and toll-gates, wharves, prisons, burial-grounds, wells etc. within the city.

His last two papers both concerned aspects of the city. *Foundations of Buildings in Hereford Castle* recorded his observations of parch marks on Castle Green, and *The Freemen's Prison at the Boothall* recorded the architectural details and historical connections of yet another historic building in the city before it was demolished.

At the Spring Annual Meeting on 11 April 1935, the president announced the death of Alfred Watkins four days earlier. George Marshall, the Honorary Secretary, reminded members of the forty-three years that Watkins had served on the central committee. During this period he had supplied more than ninety per cent of the illustrations which appeared in the *Transactions*, apart from the many valuable papers.

He was an individualist whose antiquarian researches were all made from his own personal observations and to that extent are of greater value in not relating anything from hearsay. To commemorate the memory of one of its most famous members, who had ensured by his efforts that the *Transactions* for many years had been amongst the most outstanding of such regional publications in the country, the club included a portrait of Watkins as the frontispiece in the combined volume for the years 1933 to 1935.

The Freeman's Prison which adjoined the Booth Hall in Hereford, shortly before it was demolished. This may have been the last photograph taken by Watkins (Alfred Watkins, 1934)

*The twelfth century door-knocker at Dormington Church
(Alfred Watkins, 1900)*

VIII

Ley Lines

When Watkins read a paper to members of the Woolhope Club in September 1921 he could not possibly have had any idea of the repercussions it would have throughout the whole world for the next seventy years.

His subject was innocuous enough—at least as far as the title of the talk was concerned. *Early British Trackways, Moats, Mounds, Camps and Sites* could well have been taken to be intended as a wide-ranging talk on archaeological features throughout the country-side—a subject on which the speaker was well qualified. But this was most certainly not Watkins' intention. Instead he made use of the lecture to introduce to his fellow members a totally new concept—that of 'the old straight track'.

The *Transactions* of the Woolhope Club do not give any indication of what the members present thought of this radical idea from one of their most respected and esteemed members. At the close of the meeting the president of the day merely said that the speaker 'had shown them how they could use their eyes, and he hoped they would study the subject upon which in so illuminating a manner Mr. Watkins had spoken.'

It was on 30 June 1921, when Watkins was on a chance visit to a part of the Herefordshire countryside he knew so well, that the whole idea 'came to me in a flash'.

He explained it to the meeting. 'A visit to Blackwardine led me to note on the map a straight line starting from Croft Ambrey, lying on parts of Croft Lane past the Broad (a hamlet between Leominster

123

and Luston), over hill points, through Blackwardine, over Risbury Camp, and through the high ground at Stretton Grandison, where I surmise a Roman station. I followed up the clue of sighting from hill top, unhampered by other theories, found it yielding astounding results in all districts, the straight lines to my amazement passing over and over again through the same class of objects, which I soon found to have been practical sighting points.'

He was later to describe his concept as follows: 'Imagine a fairy chain stretched from mountain peak to mountain peak, so far as the eye could reach, and paid out until it touched the high places of the earth at a number of ridges, banks and knowls. Then visualise a mound, circular earthwork, or clump of trees, planted on these high points, and in low points in the valley, other mounds ringed round with water to be seen from a distance. Then great standing stones brought to mark the way at intervals, and on a bank leading up to a mountain ridge or down to a ford the track cut deep so as to form a guiding notch on the skyline as you come up. In a bwlch or mountain pass the road cut deeply to show as a notch afar off. Here and there, and at two ends of the way, a beacon fire used to lay out the track. With ponds dug on the line or streams banked up into "flashes" to form reflecting points on the beacon track so that it might be checked when at least once a year the beacon was fired on the traditional day. All these works exactly on the sighting line.'

In essence what Watkins was suggesting was that during the whole of the prehistoric period all trackways used by traders and others followed straight lines marked out on a sighting system from hill to hill and using mark points in between. He insisted that this was demonstrated by the alignment, across miles of countryside, of a great number of objects, or sites of objects, of prehistoric antiquity—not just in a few examples but in hundreds of cases. He was to spend much of the rest of his life in accumulating evidence to demonstrate his idea and in publishing the results of his researches.

The sighting line (or ley, as it became known because of the number of places on the alignments with 'ley' in the name) needed regular marking or sighting points which could easily be seen by the user standing at the preceding point. These secondary points were the basis of Watkins' discovery, for many were objects which were marked on maps and he considered them to be acceptable if straight lines could be drawn joining four or more ancient sites. The sighting points, according to Watkins, were constructed of earth, water or stone, although trees could also have been planted on the line. The lines could be drawn through a variety of points, for the original markers, being important objects in the landscape, had subsequently been re-used and their sites marked by later, but still historic, features.

Earth sighting points included all the various types of mounds—tumuli, barrows, cairns, castle mottes, etc.—and also notches in banks or mountain ridges. Water sighting points, usually on low ground, such as moats and artificial ponds, formed a point or ring of reflection from higher ground. Mark stones were stones of various shapes and sizes, deliberately placed by the side of the track.

Iron Age camps, or hill forts as they are now usually known, often appeared on maps to be the focus of several leys which were usually aligned with the higher parts of the earthworks rather than their centre. Thus Watkins was to note with Capler Camp that it had 'so many leys over it as to seem to be the Clapham Junction of ancient trackways in that district.'

Churches or churchyard crosses, if ancient, were almost invariably to be found on one or more leys and Watkins suggested that the church or cross replaced an earlier mark stone, and pointed out the frequent coincidence of mounds or moats with early church sites. Castles, particularly those associated with mounds, also appeared on several leys, and he assumed that an earlier sighting mound was re-used as the site for a castle. It followed from this argument that 'the old straight track' decided, in the long-lost past, the site of almost every branch of human communal activity. Thus churches were often built at the crossing of two leys whilst homesteads, and eventually villages, were associated with earlier ponds or moats used as sighting points.

As a result of his researches, Watkins was convinced that the frequency of ley lines passing through historic sites used as mark points was much too common to be due solely to coincidence, and therefore his revelation was built, not just on dim folk memories, but on a carefully accumulated collection of data.

Watkins expanded his lecture to the Woolhope Club and it was published as a book entitled *Early British Trackways* in 1922, less than a year after his original discovery. He later described the book as a 'somewhat breathless production' which was sent to press only five months after he had the first clue, but it still provides the clearest exposition of his theory as it applied to Herefordshire. Apart from being the first publication on the subject of ley lines, the book has one other claim to fame—it was bound by a man called Buckridge who was later to be convicted of the murder of his wife and her foster-mother!

Ignoring the indexes, the many photographs and the two maps, there are twenty-seven pages of text. These range from a clear introduction to the subject as a whole, a definition of ley lines and the different types of sighting points (all with many examples), evidence from place-names, to hints to ley hunters and a list of several leys.

Watkins expounded on his ley line theory at every available opportunity. Thus, at a Ladies Day meeting of the Woolhope Club in 1922 at Courtfield, he described two leys which went through the mound adjacent to the mansion. He followed this with a paper in 1924 which described an alignment running from Giant's Cave, on the Eastnor side of the Malvern Hills, through a stone known as the Sacrificial Stone, thence via the churches at Woolhope and Holme Lacy, to a pond on top of the Deer Park, and then through Aconbury Church to finish at the highest point on Aconbury Camp. Not content with this remarkable alignment through no less than seven points, he also noted that both Woolhope and Holme Lacy churches were on the same exact alignment as the ley. In addition, the sun, rising above the ridge of the cave at six o'clock on Midsummers Day falls directly on the Sacrificial Stone and thus on the ley. One can well understand his wry comment 'This can scarcely be a coincidence.'

One of the most extraordinary standing stones in Herefordshire is the Queen Stone at Huntsham. It stands in the middle of a

The 'sacrificial stone' near to the Giant's Cave on the Malvern Hills.
Watkins evidently had a willing volunteer for his photograph!
(Alfred Watkins, 1924)

meadow within the horseshoe bend of the River Wye which also includes Symond's Yat. When Watkins knew it, the stone stood some 2.3m high above ground level (ploughing has since reduced the amount visible a little) with the main face 1.6m wide and the thickness 1.1m. All the sides contain deep vertical grooves, 5 to 6cm wide and up to 18cm deep.

Watkins had established from maps that the Queen Stone was a mark stone on at least three separate alignments and, because of its unusual design and position, he decided to organise an excavation around the base of the stone. This took place in September 1926, and to his surprise he found that the deep grooves all stopped abruptly at the then ground level, although about 2.4m of the stone was buried under the ground. He established from his excavations that the original hole for the stone had been dug with one straight and one sloping side and suggested that the stone had been slid in and raised against the vertical face, the base on the other side being then packed with stones before the hole was filled. Within the excavations were several worked flints, fragments of burnt bone and large quantities of charcoal.

From the design of the stone and the objects found in association with it, Watkins deduced that, apart from its use as a ley marker, it had also been used as a sacrificial stone. He suggested that long osier rods could have been placed in each groove to form a rough 'cage' or 'basket' above the stone, the whole being bound with withies. The sacrificial object would then have been put within the cage and the whole was then fired. He provides, in his article on the subject in the Woolhope Club *Transactions*, an account of a similar practice which was apparently carried out by the Druids and described in Caesar's *War in Gaul*.

Some seven years later, when he was seventy-eight years old, Watkins volunteered to give a talk on the subject to some five hundred Woodcraft Folk who were camped around the Queen Stone. This organised camp movement drew its members from the co-operative and kindred bodies, typically from the larger cities. In preparation for this talk the Woodcraft Folk built a 'cage' on the stone to Watkins' specifications, complete with two 'victims' inside.

The Queen Stone at Huntsham with its peculiar vertical grooves. This photograph was taken during the excavations arranged by Watkins and shows the amount of stone which was buried (Alfred Watkins, 1926)

*Watkins giving a talk to the Woodcraft Folk in 1933 watched by two
'victims' in a wicker cage built above the Queen Stone*

The event was captured on film—the only known cinematographic
representation of Watkins.

He followed his paper on the Queen Stone with one in 1927 on
the Wergin's Stone, some four miles north of Hereford near Sutton.
This 1.5m high stone with its roughly pentagonal base he also
considered to be a mark stone. In addition, the stone has had rather
an odd reputation, gaining the alternative name of the Devil's
Stone, for in the 1695 edition of Camden's *Britannia* it appears in
an account of what would seem to be a rather purposeless miracle.

'Between Sutton and Hereford, in a common meadow called the
Wergins, were placed two large stones for a water mark, one erected
upright, the other laid athwart. In the late civil wars, about the year
1652, they were removed to about twelve score paces distance, and
nobody knows how; which gave occasion to a common opinion that
they were carried thither by the Devil. When they were set in their
places again, one of them required nine yoke of oxen to draw it.'

A year later Watkins, still continuing his researches into mark points, read a paper to the Woolhope Club on Arthur's Stone, a well-known megalithic burial chamber which lies on top of Merbach Hill above the village of Bredwardine in west Herefordshire. He describes it in some detail and refers to earlier records of a ring of stones around the monument and also of excavations on the site. He then describes the various alignments he had discovered which went through the mound which had originally covered the stone burial chamber.

In 1925 Watkins completed what was to be his most famous book—*The Old Straight Track*. It is the only book by the author which is still in print. From the preface to the original edition the reader can get some idea of the way that Watkins saw his great idea when he commented that 'in fully half a century's familiar contact with this region my other self had, quite unknown to me, worked at one subject.' The book was the result of almost four years' strenuous

Arthur's Stone, a megalithic burial chamber on Merbach Hill above Bredwardine. Watkins established four alignments which he considered to go through the site (Alfred Watkins)

field work, all carried out during his late 60's, to provide what he considered to be the necessary evidence to prove his case.

The contents of *The Old Straight Track* follow a similar order to those in his previous book *Early British Trackways*, but with far more details on the various types of sighting points—mounds, moats, mark stones etc.—and including beacons for the first time. In chapter eleven he discusses the skilled men who originally laid out the ley lines. He based much of his evidence for these people on place names and from his studies came to the conclusion that it was the coleman who gave his name to many points and places on the tracks, and that he must have been the head-man of the team who made them. This followed from the many place names incorporating 'cole' which he found were associated with leys over the country as a whole. The surveyor was the dod-man who used two long sighting staves. He considered that this ancient surveyor was commemorated in the Long Man of Wilmington, the 240 feet long prehistoric figure, complete with two staves, cut into the turf on the hillside at Wilmington in Sussex. Finally the tenderer of the beacon, an essential part of the construction team for these were usually at the beginning of leys, was the 'black' man.

Examples in other lands, biblical references to the straight track, confirmation of leys in other parts of the British Isles and a discussion of objections to the theory all make the book compulsive reading, whilst the inclusion of over a hundred photographs (all taken by the author and mainly in Herefordshire) provide a highly visual background to the whole subject. When it was first published the reviewer in *The New Statesman* said 'Only an out-of-doors man could have written this book, and only a man with a student's critical faculty could have weighed and dovetailed the evidence here collected. It is admirably illustrated and a first-rate piece of work.'

On the whole Watkins' discovery was ignored by contemporary academic archaeologists who would not even consider the existence of ley lines and mark points and for many years were not prepared to discuss the subject. *The Old Straight Track* was considered to be so radical that the editor of the archaeological journal *Antiquity* refused to include a paid advertisement, let alone review it.

Watkins wrote only one book which detailed ley lines in an area outside his home county. This was *Archaic Tracks Round Cambridge*, published by Simkin Marshall Ltd. in 1932. He admits in his introduction that the book is only a framework for local and field investigation for the two branches of enquiry—map and field work. In the book he offers the former but leaves the field work 'to those who by health-giving tramps along the lines indicated, will, I feel sure, find new corroboration.' He indicates that the work was a result of a flying visit to Cambridge during which a glance at local maps had indicated that the district was remarkably rich in mark-point evidence. He was visiting his son, Allen, who worked in Cambridge at that time. Allen, a fervent believer in ley lines, said of the book that it had many claims to be considered the best he ever wrote, even though he only took a couple of months in both the research and the writing.

He starts the book, as he did with the two earlier ones, with a description of his discovery and then uses this as a basis for the investigation which follows. He goes on to discuss the arguments against accidental coincidence which several critics had raised. In the third chapter he describes seven alignments through the borough of Cambridge. This is expanded in chapter four where he includes a reduced version of the one-inch popular edition of the Ordnance Survey map showing a multiplicity of straight alignments all within an area of some twelve miles around Cambridge. In all, twenty-five alignments are shown and described, each with a minimum of five mark points.

He goes on to consider the origin of the most famous of the older roads in the Cambridge area—Ermine Street, Icknield Way, Akeman Street and Via Devana—and presents mark-point evidence for what he sees as their original courses before they became the straight roads that are known today.

He then discusses the possibility that some of the alignments are seasonal (e.g associated with the midsummer sunrise), that some churches are aligned on leys constructed from earlier sighting marks, and that several of the leys around Cambridge are aligned with the cardinal points of the compass. He compares the evidence for the latter theory with the cardinal point alignments he had discovered in the Radnor Forest area where they were apparently associated with cup-marked stones.

In the final chapter he mentions Dr. Cyril Fox's scholarly work *The Archaeology of the Cambridge Region*, which he had read on completion of his own work. He comments that the author 'naturally adopts the orthodox opinion (I think, wrongly), that straightness and alignment is an exclusive sign of Roman engineering, all earlier ones being sinuous. This excepted I find his attitude and information as to prehistoric tracks and their mark-points amazingly full, up-to-date, and open-minded'. He concludes his own book by apologising for the lack of photographs, which he blames on his advancing years, and hopes that others will follow up with the field work pointing out that 'adventure lies lurking in these lines where I point the way for younger feet than mine.'

It can be seen from this book that Watkins was not content to work as an individual—he wished to involve others in his researches, and in this he was extremely successful. His first serious attempt was the publication in 1927 of *The Ley Hunter's Manual*, a practical guide to early tracks. This ninety page book with some sixty-four illustrations, also published by Simkin Marshall, was well received as can be seen from the review in the Birmingham Gazette which noted: 'It is given to few people to create, even on a small scale, a new out-door hobby. That is what Mr. Watkins did by his field work and writing on leys or early British trackways.'

Some reviewers were not so kind and one, after reading *Archaic Tracks Round Cambridge*, tried a practical experiment.

'Reflecting on the instinct of the unregenerate walker to make for the nearest pub, the reviewer took the same one-inch map and, selecting inns as his sight-marks, obtained similar results to Mr. Watkins. His first, and best, effort produced six inns in line; another, four inns and the significant place name Two Pots House. Four lines of four inns can be drawn, each terminating on one of the Noon Follies (associated with Watkins' midday sighting lines); and considering the original meaning of noon—about 3 o'clock—and the impossibility of obtaining a drink at that hour, the result is no doubt significant and our English road system is to be attributed to Mr. Watkins' sight-walker, gradually developing into Mr. Chesterton's reeling English drunkard.'

Such criticism did not unduly worry Watkins and indeed he continued to emphasise that ley hunting gave a new zest to field rambles. In *Early British Trackways* he had a mental vision of a scout-master of the future instructing his troops—'Now we have found the ley, I think we shall see a bit of the old track in that far grassy field this side the moat; it's narrow and straight, and there are many who never find it because they look for a broad way like our present wheel tracks.'

In 1926 Watkins helped in the formation of The Straight Track Club, a loose organisation of interested amateurs who circulated news of their discoveries through a series of postal portfolios. The club held a three days' meeting in Hereford in 1933. At this time Watkins was the president of the new group and he arranged a joint meeting with the Woolhope Club where he spoke on *A Sacrificial Stone at Lydney.*

The Straight Track Club continued its activities until the mid 1940's, some ten years after Watkins died. The 41 portfolios, papers, photographs and maps, which had been gathered over the years, eventually ended up in Hereford library, where they are still regularly consulted by ley-hunters.

In 1945 The Avalon Society attempted to take over from The Straight Track Club and continue their work, but interest in the subject dwindled during the late 1940's and early 1950's. This was changed in 1958 when Aime Michel's book *Flying Saucers and the Straight Line Mystery* was published in France. This suggested that Unidentified Flying Object flight paths could be associated with Watkins' straight tracks. The theory was expanded in *Skyways and Landmarks* by Tony Wedd, published in 1961 and reprinted in 1972.

The revival of interest which followed these publications led to the formation of The Ley Hunters Club. The first public meeting was held on Saturday 17 November 1962 in Kensington Central Library when Allen Watkins spoke about his father's early work under the title The History of Ley Study. Between 1965 and 1967 some eight issues of the club magazine *The Ley Hunter* were published. Several articles by John Michell in the underground publication *International Times* followed which led to the publication of his major work *The View Over Atlantis* in 1969. Michell elaborated on an alternative theory for ley lines, first suggested by Arthur Lawton in the Straight Track Club's portfolio for 1927. Lawton had considered that leys marked a network of a subtle form of energy which could be detected by dowsing. Michell elaborated on this theory, suggesting that ancient man knew and utilised this form of energy but that the knowledge and methods had since been lost.

Michell's book ushered in a new wave of interest in the possible relationships between ley lines, astronomical data and terrestrial lines of current. Paul Screeton took over the editorship of *The Ley Hunter* which re-emerged in 1969 in a much improved form.

The ley hunters returned to Hereford for a field meeting on 3 July 1971, to celebrate the 50th anniversary of Watkins' discovery of leys. Once again his son Allen gave a talk to the assembled members and this must have brought back some memories for the meeting was held in the Woolhope Club room. The party then moved on to Risbury Camp, one of the mark points on the line of the first ley to be discovered by Watkins, where they held a picnic.

The Ley Hunter magazine is still published and has a loyal band of followers. Although they reach out to all the various branches of fringe science, they still draw on the early ideas of Alfred Watkins and his primary and, still, the best researched pioneering writings in this field.

IX

Public Service

Watkins had a strong sense of public duty which manifested itself in many ways.

In politics he was a traditional Liberal, being one of many idealists during the latter part of the nineteenth century. However, he always protested against the inclusion of party politics in local elections. He was in favour of votes for women and felt that the farm worker—the salt of the earth—had had a poor deal throughout history.

In the early twentieth century he supported Free Trade rather than Chamberlain's ideas on protective tariffs and was so concerned about the subject that he spent much time travelling around the county giving lantern-lecture talks to local villagers. From time to time Watkins took his young son with him and Allen recalled the meetings as seeing 'English history at first hand.' The young Allen felt that the meetings, which were all well attended, had a considerable political effect.

At the beginning of the First World War, Watkins was responsible for organising almost one hundred recruiting meetings and became the military representative on the Hereford Recruiting Tribunal. This was the local organisation which decided whether people applying for postponement of conscription on business or personal grounds had a legitimate case. It was a post which would have kept him busy throughout the war.

The preservation of law and order and the fair administration of justice was of great importance to the true liberal. Watkins, with his strong sense of public duty, became a county magistrate in 1907 and served on the Bench for many years.

He entered the local political arena in 1914 when he became county councillor for the Tupsley division of the city. By this time his children had grown up and he had ceased to be involved on a day-by-day basis with his various business enterprises. He must have felt that he could now devote sufficient time to local affairs to justify standing for the council, and continued to represent Tupsley until, a year before his death, he was made a county alderman.

All people who are active in the local political field are expected to take on many other responsibilities besides the obvious one of attending the main council meetings. Watkins was no exception, and was a member of the finance, education, and stage play and cinematograph licences committees. Some of his other voluntary activities included being a governor of both the local high schools and for many years the chairman of the committee of the School of Arts and Crafts. He may well have achieved a long service record in his membership of the Hereford City Council's library committee, on which he served from 1880 to 1934 as a co-opted member. He was also a member of the education committee and was involved with the Old House committee from its inception.

The executive committee responsible for the erection of the county and city War Memorial in St. Peter's Square held all their deliberations under Watkins' chairmanship, and he must have had considerable influence both on the type of memorial and the choice of site.

In 1902 he was appointed a trustee of the Hereford Municipal Charities and rendered much valuable service to this body for some thirty-three years.

Watkins was a regular contributor to the Hereford Times with letters, articles and photographs. Many of these were reports of recent archaeological discoveries, but several were critical of the decisions made and, in some cases, of the lack of resolute action by the city council.

In a typical example Watkins wrote to protest about a proposal to change the name of Bewell Street. 'It always has been a mean street,

The War Memorial in St. Peter's Square, Hereford. Watkins chaired the committee which selected this Eleanor Cross (Ken Hoverd, 1990)

but it was an adjoining lane which had an especially unsavoury reputation, and this the city fathers, without the faintest result, tried to sweeten by calling it another name. Now even supposing (I don't say it is) that a nest of sinners is to be found in Bewell Street, the fact won't be altered by calling it All Saints Street.'

Hereford lost a certain amount of atmosphere when those in power decided to abandon the ancient street names. Amongst others, Commercial Street replaced Bye Street within the Gate; East Street and West Street were new names for Packers Lane; Union Street was used instead of Gaol Lane; Aubrey Street for Wroughthall Lane, and we must thank Watkins for saving Bewell Street at least.

In the early 1930's Watkins was concerned about an important aspect of the traffic problems in the city—this was many years before the city walls ring road was built and at that time all traffic travelling east and west through the city had to pass through the narrow High Street. In an article in the Hereford Times, illustrated by his contemporary photograph of the re-building of the shop immediately to the east of All Saints Church (now part of Boots), he expresses his regret of what he saw as a lost opportunity.

139

'It brings up mournful thoughts of past neglect of citizens' interests by the city council, and visions of "what might have been" if there had been a little more looking ahead.

'If only when the Town Planning Act gave powers some twenty years ago, preparations had been made for a bold plan for the removal of the whole block of houses lying between High Street and Bewell Street so that the wide High Town would be extended up to All Saints Church, the gain to citizens would in the long run far outweigh the cost, which would be largely met by the new shop frontages created in Bewell Street. If this were accomplished Eign Street and Bewell Street would become one-way streets, and the present felt need of making Eign Street wider, alleviated.

'Lover of picturesque buildings as I am, I must say that the removal of the old Town Hall has secured for Hereford the first place in comparison with Worcester and Gloucester for being a bright, open city.'

He concludes his article on past failures by regretting that the city council was not taking the opportunity created by the demolition to 'open out a through walking-way against the east end of All Saints, and thus restore to the community what was obviously stolen from them some generations back.'

Watkins' 'bold plan' may well have alleviated the city traffic for a few years, but would eventually have had to be superseded by modern plans to separate pedestrians from motor traffic as far as possible.

He achieved something on this latter line when, in 1893, the footpath which runs along the north bank of the River Wye below the grounds of the General Hospital was opened, largely due to his efforts.

But his sense of public service and duty extended beyond the area of politics and civic affairs. The Hereford Rowing Club had been established in 1861 after several successful but informally organised regattas. Watkins is first mentioned as a member in 1878 when he was in the team which came second for the Corporation Plate. He took part in many events and at the 1883 Annual General Meeting was appointed to the managing committee. He soon

The new path below the grounds of the general hospital before the suspension bridge was built (Alfred Watkins, 1896)

became the captain of the club and in 1885, when the club had an excursion to Sugwas, with twenty-two members in 3-pair oared boats and twenty-two more in double-sculled boats, he provided a 'capital spread' as a reward for their exertions. He was still captain when the club decided to build a new club-house in 1887 but was replaced in the early 1890's, probably due to his age and increasing family commitments. The club members put their own efforts into improving the club-house and brought stone down the river from Belmont rapids in a large punt belonging to Jordans (who operated hire boats on the river) to construct new steps from the club-house to the river. Watkins recorded this work in a series of photographs which are still displayed in the club-house. Despite relinquishing the captaincy he retained a close association with the club throughout his life, becoming a vice-president in 1901.

He continued to have a wide variety of interests and was one of the founders of the Hereford Debating Society, as well as a member of the committee of the Herefordshire Historical Association on its re-formation in 1926.

He also had a long standing interest in bees and bee-keeping, and late in the nineteenth century he produced a series of lantern slides on the subject. The slides were accompanied with a booklet which he also wrote on *Bees and Bee-keeping* for a series called *Optical Lantern Readings*. The booklet lists and describes some thirty slides including some which, at that time, would have been difficult to photograph. They included 'The abdomen of the worker bee' and 'The antenna comb on the first leg' both of which must have been taken using a microscope.

It was always the responsibility of the retiring president of the Woolhope Club to provide an address to the members at the spring meeting following their term of office. In 1919, after his presidential year, Watkins decided that, rather than offer an archaeological subject, he would take as a topic 'the one natural-history subject on which I am sufficiently qualified to speak, that of the only insect which we in the British Isles subserve to the use of man—namely the Honey Bee'. He described, with photographs, the history of the honey bee and its importance after the Norman Conquest when the Domesday Survey records Welsh tenants in Archenfield as paying their dues in honey; the methods of early local bee-keeping and the various types of hives; how to retain swarms and aspects of the law relating to bees. The latter he found rather fascinating because of the fundamental differences in English law between wild and domesticated animals. Bees do not necessarily fit into these cosy categories. Thus, as Watkins noted 'When bees swarm, it is a toss up whether they settle within their owner's reach and remain his property, or make a bolt for it and become either free or the property of whoever may hive them.'

In 1882, Watkins was a member of the founding committee of the Herefordshire Bee-Keepers Association and was its secretary until 1901. The association held an annual honey fair in Hereford for about eighteen years and organised a bee-tent at local flower and agricultural shows. The association ceased to operate about 1904, but a new one was formed shortly afterwards and is still in existence.

During the years of the depression towards the end of the nineteenth century, the association took on a public role by attempting

Alfred Watkins gathering a swarm of bees

to popularise and teach good and efficient bee-keeping. This was achieved by means of a horse-drawn bee van which toured the county. The bee van was the subject of the last slide in his lecture series and of this he said in the accompanying text 'In Herefordshire, the county council, recognising the importance of spreading information on the subject, have granted sufficient funds to send a bee van from village to village, the instructor giving practical demonstrations in some bee-keeper's garden. As shades of night begin to fall the pictures ... are shown on a screen filling up the end of the van.'

An anonymous article about the bee van appeared in the *Pall Mall Budget* in 1892. It well illustrates the problems of imparting technical information on the subject to a rural population in the latter part of the nineteenth century. The magic lantern helped to draw in the audience and the results, if not immediately spectacular, were considered to be of long term benefit as hives and systems were gradually improved. The article is written as if by a fly on the wall.

'"I don't believe in your new-fangled ways" explains one old bee-keeper, "I get along very comfortably without". "But how do you take the honey?" asks the expert. "Well. I lights a bit of sulphur and brown paper and puts it under the hive at night time". "And do you get any sleep that night?" demands the instructor pointedly; and the man has to admit that he does feel some qualms after murdering the whole colony of tiny workers who have laboured so hard during the summer to lay by their winter food supply, and he finally promises to try the improved system.'

Watkins' fertile mind also took him into what we might consider strange avenues. One of his most unusual published works, issued through the Watkins Meter Company, should perhaps have been reprinted in the late 1960's.

Must We Trade In Tenths was in fact published in 1919, just after the end of the Great War. Watkins described it as 'a plea against decimal and for octaval coinage as more exactly fitting the wants and usage of all who make, grow, buy or sell things.' For at this time there were proposals to convert to a decimal currency based on

The Bee Van attracting a rather sceptical looking audience
(Alfred Watkins)

1,000 mils to £1 (inflation 50 years later made this 100 pence to £1!). Watkins was fiercely opposed to this proposal and went into considerable detail in his booklet to demonstrate that his ideas were superior to those being proposed.

His basic philosophy was that for trading purposes it would be much more convenient if currency, weights and measures were based on the series 2, 4, 8, 16, 32 etc, and the corresponding fractions of a half, quarter, eighth and so on, allowing divisions up and down to the unit 1. The fatal defect of the decimal system, as Watkins saw it, was that 10 only halves to five—a prime number.

The pre-decimal currency consisted of twelve pence to a shilling and twenty shillings to a pound. The coins above the shilling were the florin (two shillings or one-tenth of a pound, first issued in 1849 so that people might 'get educated to decimals') and the half-crown (two shillings and six pence). The half-crown was one-eighth of a pound and was the basis of Watkins' new currency.

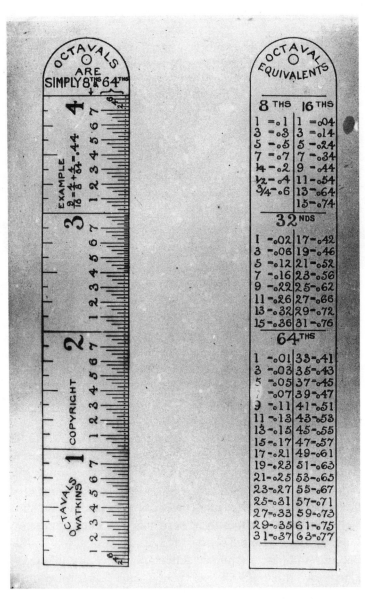

'Octavals are simply 8ths and 64ths.' Octaval equivalents
as suggested by Watkins (Alfred Watkins)

He proposed an octaval system consisting of:

Eight cents to one groat

Eight groats to one half-crown

Eight half-crowns to one pound

leaving the half-crown and the pound unaltered. The coinage would have been in multiples of 4, 2 and 1 of each unit below the pound, each coin being half the value of the previous in an unbroken series down to its 512th part—the cent, being an approximate equivalent to the old half-penny of which there were 480 to the pound.

To make this system work on a continuous series of numbers similar to decimals (rather than fractions) the digits 8 and 9 would not have been used in this coinage, except for full pounds. Carrying out mathematical operations would have been interesting to say the least! Thus, using an * as the octaval mark to separate whole pounds from octaval fractions, addition would have appeared as follows:

$$
\begin{array}{r}
\text{£} \\
5{*}04 \\
16{*}721 \\
1{*}5 \\
\underline{29{*}662} \\
53{*}343
\end{array}
$$

The final column adds up to 3 cents which is put down; the next column gives 12 groats which makes one 8 with 4 left over which is again put down. Carrying over the 8 groats which is 1 half-crown to the column to the right of * adds to 19 half-crowns—two 8s with 3 left over. The 3 is written down and the 2 pounds carried over to the pounds column to the left of * which is then added up in the normal way in a ten grouping. The result is read as 53 pounds, 3 half-crowns, 4 groats and 3 cents.

Multiplication is also a new adventure:

$$
\begin{array}{r}
\text{£}54{*}361 \\
\underline{\times 6} \\
\text{£}326{*}646
\end{array}
$$

In this case 6 times 1 is 6, which being less than 8 is put down. 6 times 6 is 36, which is four 8s and 4 over, the latter put down. 6 times 3 is 18 which, with the 4 half-crowns carried over is 22. This contains two 8s, i.e £2, which is carried over and 6 left, again put down. The £54 to the left of * is multiplied by 6 in the usual way in tens, adding in the £2 carried over.

Watkins envisaged similar changes to weights and measures and quoted many examples where his system was partly in use. The inch divided, as it still is on rulers, into eighths; eight gills to a pint and eight pints to a gallon. His system had merit—an octaval coinage would have been much easier for shopkeepers giving change; the Stock Exchange fractions of 64ths of £1 would have been simplified to £0*01 as opposed to £0.015625, and paper sizes would have been a half of the preceding size. Watkins also saw its advantage in photography where exposure times are easier to follow when in octaval fractions allowing each to be one-half of the next above.

The booklet, now long out of print, sold for three pence—had there been octaval currency this would have been approximately one groat, or eight cents.

He continued his battle against the proposed decimal currency in a letter to *The Nation* (a liberal journal) where he was supported by no less a figure than George Bernard Shaw.

X

The Final Years

After their two children had left home Alfred and Marion Watkins
decided to move into a smaller house closer to the centre of the city.
In 1919 they found the requisite spot at 5 Harley Court, less than a
hundred yards from the cathedral but still in a quiet, secluded situation. The building, facing onto a narrow passagēway which joins the
Cathedral Close to the rear of the town hall, is of brick and appears
to be of eighteenth century date. But this facade, although pleasant
in its own right, hides a much earlier, timber-framed building.

One of the first receptions which they hosted in their new home
was for members of the Woolhope Club who were invited to visit
after their tour around the medieval walls of the city on 25
September 1919. Marion Watkins provided tea and her husband,
president for that year, read a paper to the visitors about three of
the earliest timber-framed halls in Hereford. The third of these was
the hall in his new house at Harley Court where they were then
sitting. At that time a false ceiling completely hid the timber roof,
but Watkins had obtained a drawing, made by W.W. Robinson who
had superintended repairs to the building in 1884, of the room and
its roof. The hall, with its finely decorated roof-timbers, was probably built in the first half of the fifteenth century for one of the
canons at the cathedral. The false ceiling has since been removed
and the roof timbers are now visible.

Watkins was not the sort of person who could retire and quietly
tend his garden. Although he was sixty-four when he moved to
Harley Court he continued to be involved with his photographic

5 Harley Court, the Watkins' home from 1919 to 1935
(Ken Hoverd, 1990)

business; he attended the regular meetings of the many official bodies to which he had been elected; he spent much time with the affairs of the Woolhope Club and the Straight Track Club; and, on top of all this, found time to write new books and articles about his recently discovered ley lines.

His son, Allen, eventually married and in 1920 a grandson, Felix, was born. Felix still remembers 'kissing a rather prickly gentleman, who was clearly glad to see me, but who almost at once disappeared into his sanctum at the top of the stairs.' From time to time he went out with his grandfather in his car—then a Jowett, for steam cars were no longer available—stopping at ancient sites, inevitably to take photographs, and visiting an excavation where the young Felix proudly dug up a piece of pottery. With Felix, as with all of us, it is the small things which always linger in his memory from childhood—walking across High Town with grandfather to a shop where parts were bought for his Hornby model railway, or watching with awe the arrival of a policeman at Harley Court, probably there on magistrate's business.

A sketch by W.W. Robinson in 1884 of the early fifteenth century timber roof of the hall at 5 Harley Court (Alfred Watkins)

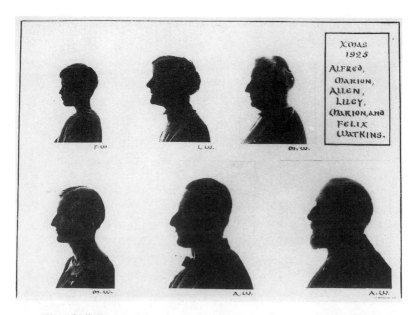

The 1925 Watkins' family Christmas card with silhouettes of all the family—Alfred bottom right and his wife Marion above; son Allen with his wife Lucy above; daughter Marion and grandson Felix (Alfred Watkins)

One mealtime he remembers his grandfather pushed away a potted plant which was inhibiting him carving the meat. '"They're very nice", said my grandmother, "they're begonias." To which Watkins replied "Begone Begonias!"'

Watkins' son Allen remembered a poem which his father often used to recite, and which was subsequently written down in a family scrapbook.

> Bloaters and bats for breakfast,
> Sparrows and sprats for tea,
> New milk in vats
> For respectable cats,
> Industrious cats like me

Rabbits and rats for dinner,
Mice and their brats for tea,
Best butter pats
For respectable cats,
Industrious cats like me.

The last fifteen years of Watkins' life were fully occupied with the affairs of the city and county he knew so well. He continued to take a keen interest in all matters of historical importance in Hereford and the surrounding areas, recording and photographing them with his accustomed flair and with little thought for his own health. Thus he neglected an internal problem and eventually fell ill in the middle of 1934. After some nine months of illness he died at his home on 7 April 1935.

A fancy dress ball at the School of Art about 1930. Watkins was Chairman of the Governors and took part in events (he is seated second from the right). The young girl in the front was eventually to marry Watkins' grandson

The funeral service took place three days later in the cathedral's Lady Chapel, with the dean, Rev. Dr. R. Waterfield, officiating. Apart from the family mourners, practically every organisation with which Watkins had been associated was represented; many members of both the city and county council also attended and the Lady Chapel was full to capacity. Prior to the service the organist played The Angel's Farewell from The Dream of Gerontius and, at the conclusion, the tragic opening notes from Chopin's Funeral March. At this precise moment, as his son recollected many years later, '... the sun broke through the clouds for the first time that day and sunshine flooded the aisles of the cathedral as we slowly filed out ...'

He left all his photographic equipment and negatives to Mr. Mckaig, who had been manager of the Meter Works, but who himself died shortly afterwards. Subsequently the photographic negatives and prints consisting of some 3,500 items were obtained by Hereford library, where they can be viewed. Much of the photographic equipment eventually passed to Hereford City Museum.

Watkins also left to what was then the Hereford Free Public Library, a number of his books, and these, mainly on bee-keeping, are still maintained as a separate collection.

His obituary filled two columns of the Hereford Times and was headed Death of World Famous Herefordian. The writer, who had been a friend for some twenty years, asked 'Who in the city can be unfamiliar with that slightly bent figure: intense, abrupt, hurrying to some business or engaged in animated conversation, oblivious to anything save the object in hand.'

He could not have described Watkins better. 'Under his brusque manner lay a nature kindly, generous and just. All will miss him, and with his passing goes a landmark in Hereford life and history. All his life was spent here; rarely leaving it even for holidays, he loved the villages, lanes, churches, hills and mounds, explored and photographed the county from end to end, and had an intimate knowledge of its physical details which few others can have achieved without such a lifelong affection.

'First and foremost he was a Herefordshire man, as native to the county as the hop and the apple.'

His death was not just an item for the local paper; The Daily Express, then a slightly more sober paper than it is today, recorded in its leaderette on 9 April under the heading Just Citizen 'A good citizen died yesterday—the kind which keeps the public life of the countryside on the highest plane of any in the world.

'His name was Alfred Watkins. You can conjure with it in Herefordshire and the counties of the Welsh Border. He was scholar, miller, archaeologist, naturalist, inventor, magistrate, County Councillor, politician, and leader of public opinion. He was full of years and honours.

'You could say of him what (the) Earl of Morton said at the graveside of John Knox "Here lies one who never feared nor flattered any flesh".'

Bibliography

This bibliography of Alfred Watkins' published work is split into several sections for convenience of use. The first lists books and pamphlets, the second a chronological list of his contributions to the Woolhope Club *Transactions*. No attempt has been made to include articles where Watkins' contribution was purely photographic—after all, this would include the great majority of the articles in the *Transactions* for a considerable period of time! The final section, doubtless incomplete, lists other known published articles.

Books and Pamphlets

A Survey of Pigeon Houses in Herefordshire and in Gower (Royal Archaeological Journal, 1891, vol. xlviii, p29, and then published in a limited edition of 75 copies by William Pollard and Co., Exeter, for private distribution)

The Watkins Manual of Exposure and Development (Watkins Meter Co. and Simkin Marshall Ltd., 1894, with 10 further editions)

Photography: its Principles and Applications (Constable and Co., 1911, with 2 further editions)

Must we trade in Tenths? (Watkins Meter Co., 1919)

Early British Trackways (Watkins Meter Co. and Simkin Marshall Ltd., 1922)

The Old Straight Track (Methuen & Co. Ltd., 1925, with 3 further editions; Garnstone Press Ltd., 1970, Abacus 1974, with several further editions)

The Ley-Hunters' Manual (Simkin Marshall Ltd., 1927)

The Old Standing Crosses of Herefordshire (Woolhope Naturalists' Field Club & Simkin Marshall Ltd., 1930)

Archaic Tracks around Cambridge (Simkin Marshall & Co. Ltd., 1932)

Guide to the Old House, Hereford (Old House Committee, Hereford City Council, 1934)

Transactions of the Woolhope Naturalists' Field Club

1890-92 *Herefordshire Pigeon-houses* (pp9-22 and 6pp illustrations)
1895-97 *The Earthquake of December 17th, 1896* (pp228-35 and plan)
1902-04 *Offa's Dyke: The Gap in the Weobley District* (pp246-250)
   Additional Notes on Pigeon-houses (pp264-5)
1912-13 *Supposed Subterraneous Passage near Hereford* (pp26-30)
1914-17 *The Strange Story of Wisteston Chapel* (pp25-29)
   Herefordshire Churchyard Crosses (pp114-19)
   Herefordshire Wayside and Town Crosses (pp249-60)
   An Ancient Herefordshire Pottery (pp280-81)
1918-20 Presidential Address: *Bees and Bee-keeping* (ppLXXI-LXXVII)
   Hereford City Walls (pp159-63)
   Three Early Timber Halls in the City of Hereford (pp164-71)
   Roaring Meg (pp172-74)
   The Brooks Called Eign (pp175-7)
   Garway Church (pp206-8)
   The King's Ditch of the City of Hereford (pp249-58)
1921-23 *Two Hereford Trackways* (pp174-5)
1924-26 *Alignment of Giant's Cave and Sacrificial Stone, Malvern Hills* (pp8-9)
   Report on a Pottery Site at Lingen (pp76-78)

Archaeology Reports

All the annual parts of the *Transactions* from 1917 to 1934 contain an Annual Archaeological Report by Watkins

Other Articles

Hereford, Herefordshire and The Wye, 1882 (written by D.R. Chapman but illustrations taken from photographs by Watkins who also assisted in compiling the walks)

Paper on *Exposure* in The British Journal of Photography, 1890

Factorial Method of Development, 1894

Animal Photography Field Naturalists Quarterly, May 1902

Record Photography Field Naturalists Quarterly, August 1902

A Summer amongst the Dovecots The English Illustrated Magazine, undated

Bees and Bee-keeping Optical Lantern Readings, undated

Also from Logaston Press

Aspects of Herefordshire, by Andrew Johnson & Stephen Punter
Aspects of Worcestershire, by Andrew Johnson & Stephen Punter
Ludford Bridge and Mortimer's Cross, by Geoffrey Hodges
The Humble-bee Its Life History and How to Domesticate it, by F.W.L. Sladen
The Happy Farmers, by Sheila Wenham
Walks & More (revised edition), by Andrew Johnson & Stephen Punter